Requiem for a
Spanish Village

BARBARA NORMAN

STEIN AND DAY/*Publishers*/New York

First published in 1972
Copyright © 1972 by Barbara Norman
Library of Congress Catalog Card No. 72-82853
All rights reserved
Published simultaneously in Canada by Saunders of Toronto, Ltd.
Designed by Bernard Schleifer
Printed in the United States of America
Stein and Day/*Publishers*/ 7 East 48 Street, New York, N.Y. 10017
ISBN 0-8128-1522-X

❧ Contents

᪥ Introduction

GOING BACK to the land, back to nature, to life on an island or in an old-fashioned village—these are dreams many of us have had as we ride on subways, drive on speedways, and live in sooty cities or isolated suburbs. Old-fashioned village life still existed in Spain when my husband and I went to live there in 1961. Today village life is changing so rapidly that it will probably soon vanish altogether. Indeed, all Spain changed faster in the decade we lived there than it had in the past five centuries.

Spain's age-old isolation has ended. Almost every book about the country points out in the first chapter, if not on the first page, that Spain and the Spaniard have always remained apart from the rest of Europe, cut off from the Continent symbolically and physically by the Pyrenees, the 10,000-foot-high barrier that crosses the entire top of the Iberian peninsula. That ancient barrier has been broken in the last decade, not by conquest but by the peaceful invasion of tourists, whose numbers swelled to 14 million a year by the mid-1960's and over 24 million in 1970, or approximately three tourists for every four Spaniards.

The tourist boom swept over Spain and its half-dormant economy like a floodtide, as if the Pyrenees were a dam that had broken. Is it surprising that many lost their footing in the wave of speculation that followed the flood? So much was needed all at once: more hotels to lodge the invaders; factories to produce construction material; machines for the factories; distilleries, dry cleaners, laundries, restaurants, furniture, hotel equipment, food; more trucks to transport all these goods; more highways for the trucks and for the tourists' cars that are sometimes blocked at the Franco-Spanish frontier in lines stretching twenty-five miles, waiting to get into Spain. And that was not all. Close behind the tourists' demands came the demands of Spaniards, suddenly earning more and buying, buying, buying—television sets, clothes, new furniture, new plumbing, luxuries to wear, use, and eat; and cars, above all, cars.

Under the pressure of these demands, inefficiency and unproductiveness, once a way of life, are no longer viable. The first years we lived in the village, I watched a thin, wiry old man toiling all day, every day, in the hot sun cutting the roadside weeds with a scythe along the six miles from the village to the nearest market town. It was an unending task. By the time he had cleared the sixth mile, the weeds had grown back at the beginning of his route, and he had to start over again. My neighbors smiled and shrugged. There was not enough work to go around and labor was cheap. It keeps him busy, they said. Today the inefficiency of Spanish labor (and much of the charm of Spanish life) has been outmoded by spiraling demands, rising labor costs, and the pressure of competition. In consequence, every aspect of Spanish life is being transformed, and even the most remote village, after surviving centuries of wars, revolutions, famine, plague, and drought, is now threatened with extinction.

8

Although Las Casas del Torrente is merely a small, poor pueblo in a distant countryside, it takes on significance and poignancy as a mirror of the struggle between old and new that is enveloping Spain. Places, names, and events have been disguised to protect identities, but the facts and circumstances are real, and the story is true, accurately reflecting Spain today.

Spain is largely rural. Village life is far more typical than city life, yet it is an aspect of the country the casual visitor never sees. What is there to see? A few dusty streets, a church of some age but no particular artistic significance, a school, some shops, a café, a square, perhaps a fountain, and houses in rows, touching each other, presenting a solid front of whitewashed walls. Even if you drive very slowly to allow children and dogs to scurry out of the way and women seated in their doorways to drag their chairs inside, you can go through all six streets of Las Casas del Torrente in less than a minute, but you would know little more about the village than you did before. Indeed, you would never know this or any other village unless you became part of it.

In 1961, my husband, a concert violinist, and I, a freelance writer, were free to live wherever we chose, providing mail and telegrams could reach us. We chose one of the cool, white mud and stone houses in one of the thousands of small agricultural villages that dot the valleys and foothills of the northeast coast of Spain. During the ten years we lived there, we became part of our village. We were foreigners, always, but accepted. "They're not tourists, they *live* here," our neighbors would explain when introducing us.

This book is the story of the village as I saw it, being part of it, witnessing birth, death, and, above all, change. We had settled in the village seeking the past with its peace and stability. Here in the remote interior of a country long

9

isolated from the rest of Europe by geography, character, and history, we thought the past would last out our lifetimes. Instead, we came just in time to see the transformation that meant the end of countless villages in Spain, among them Las Casas del Torrente itself.

1

A House

CLOSING STILL another suitcase, I glanced across the sitting room to the patchwork of tilled fields in the shadow of pine-covered peaks turning red in a brilliant sunset. It would be another clear, sunny day tomorrow. Tomorrow, I thought sadly, I will be far away. Orange, red, and pink rays flooded the room through the open balcony doors, warming the stark whitewashed walls, flushing the clay floor tiles rose. Through the arched windows, each pine tree on the mountains stood out sharply separate in the clear, still air.

The house gave me a feeling of timelessness. A house centuries old imparts something of the rhythm of another age. How old our house was, I did not know. Two hundred years? Three hundred years? It was hard to say because, for centuries, until fifteen or twenty years ago, all village houses were built exactly the same way. What is known about the village goes back no farther than the memory of someone's grandmother, or what she remembers of what her own grandmother said. Often when I asked how old a house was, I was told, "It's very old. It was there when my grandmother was a child and no one knows when it was built."

An unusual occurrence, such as a snowstorm in April, would be qualified as something that "never happened in the memory of my grandmother," meaning that, so far as anyone could determine, it had never happened before at all. The villagers took little interest in the distant past of Las Casas. "Las Casas is nothing, nothing ever happened here," they always said. Soon, I thought now, it would be truly nothing at all, just a ruin, and the rosy tiles of our sitting room that had been worn smooth by countless generations might never be walked on again.

Already there was a strange silence. At this hour, when we first moved into the house, we used to hear carts creaking home from the fields surrounding the village, the sounds of their wheels echoing off the mountainsides and carrying the message of their homecoming for miles. The families, like the dogs, distinguished one cart from another by the sound as they waited for the men to come home to supper. They listened more and more intently as dark fell, and the noises of the village and the smell of wood smoke from cooking fires rose into the cool night air under brilliant stars.

Throughout the day I was aware of a rhythm ebbing and flowing in the village, from the moment the first mule-drawn cart rumbled by our house before daybreak to the last returning for supper after dark. As we stayed through one year, and then a second, I came to feel the rhythm of the seasons and of the work the seasons dictated, a pattern repeated year after year. In a world of change and rapid pace, there is reassurance in that slow repetition. When you live in a village so closely linked to the past, as we did, time takes on a different meaning. You come to understand the resignation, calm, and common sense of the peasant who was born within walking distance of the cemetery, who lives in a house with three generations, where he, his father, his grandfather, and his great-grandfather were born.

Now the rhythm had been broken. The peasant's children

would not be born in his house; he himself would not live there, for we were not alone in leaving. Many had left, and those remaining would soon follow. Our house, like all the others, was sturdy enough to survive centuries if lived in, but once neglected would fall into ruins. The roof tiles would cave in, the ceiling beams would sag, the two-foot-thick walls would crack, lean perilously over the dusty streets, then crumble, releasing rocks and boulders onto the abandoned fields below.

There would be no record of the village at all. No one has kept any written history of Las Casas, and what might have been eked out from property records was destroyed in 1936 when the Republicans took all the town records out of the registry office in Riera, painstakingly loaded them into carts, drove them outside the town, and burned every scrap. It took them several days, and no one knows why they did it. All that was lost was the record of ancient ownership, and we, who were probably the last owners our house would have, would never know who the first were, or when they had built it so well, so beautifully, so sturdily.

The house and the village were doomed. I only wished I could pack the timelessness, calm, and resignation they had given me in the trunks and suitcases that would carry our belongings out the door.

We had had no intention of buying a house in Las Casas del Torrente or elsewhere in Spain, or anywhere at all, for that matter. We were living in Paris, which suited us well except that from time to time the cloudy northern skies would begin to weigh upon us. Then we would drive south across the Pyrenees to the brilliant blue skies and hot sun of the Mediterranean.

It was in December of 1960 that we first visited Las Casas del Torrente, a name that might be translated as The Houses of the River, though it lacks cadence in English.

13

There were eight of us, Americans and Spaniards, men and women, on a drive from Barcelona to a region famous for its red wine and particularly for the strength of it, some 16% alcohol without fortification, or so it is claimed, at least. By chance we stopped in Las Casas, one of the villages of that region, where we spotted a rustic café just off the winding secondary road that had taken us through foothills covered with patches of almonds, olives, walnuts, and grapes, and over mountain passes blanketed with pine, thyme, and rosemary.

With dry local ham and bitter black olives, the wine was warming and welcome that cold December day. Our appetites had been sharpened by a half-hour's walk around the village, during which we admired its cut stone doorways, overhanging balconies, steep streets with precipitous views of mountains, and its tranquillity, seemingly undisturbed for centuries. People we passed on the street greeted us with smiles as if pleased we had stopped to visit.

"If you wanted a house here, you could buy one for very little," remarked Señor Pedro as he fetched wine of another year from the café cellar for us to try.

"Are there any for sale?" one of us asked idly. The thought was attractive at the moment, perhaps partly because the wine was so good. There was, in fact, and Señor Pedro would be delighted to close the café and be our guide. Why not have a look?

Although the sun was brilliant, the wind hurtled down the canyonlike streets stronger than before. We were glad to reach the house, where a large German shepherd, young and well fed, gave us a friendly greeting after some dutiful barking to alert the household. Inside, away from the sun, the clear brisk air turned dank and penetrating. The mud and stone walls and tile floor exuded cold.

"Here she comes," said our guide.

Down the narrow staircase into the mean small entrance

came a woman, half waddling, half scampering, preceded by a torrent of words.

"Aiee, and what could you want? . . . Oh, it's you, yes, about the house. Well, he's asleep, went to sleep before lunch, he's in the bedroom, and what are we to do, I don't know . . ."

We mumbled that we would come back, that there was no need to wake anyone up, that we did not want to disturb her or her husband.

"Ay, no, no, now you've come—he says from far away, from where? France? No? America! So far away! Come along . . . Ah, this house, it's the death of me." She charged up the stairs, pausing on the landing to open a door which turned out to lead to a closet. "There's closets everywhere, full of clothes," she called over her shoulder, beginning to rummage in a trunk, throwing clothes on the floor, shaking her head and looking up at us from time to time. "There's so many things here, good things and old ones . . . Look! Here's the dress my grandmother was baptized in!" She shook it in the air and threw it back in the trunk, shoved the lid shut, shrugged her shoulders, and sighed, "Ah, this house! It's too much for me, nothing but work, work, work . . . Come . . ."

We had to avoid looking at each other for fear of laughing. We trooped up two flights of narrow stairs to an unused third floor, where she had us inspect a primitive toilet in a long corridor, three unfurnished rooms, one with no windows, and several hallways where racks of clothing hung under dusty sheets, which she whipped on and off as if we were to buy a flea market of clothes along with the house. All the while she spouted a stream of derogatory comments about its condition.

"The roof has to be repaired, it's in very bad shape, leaks when it rains. And all this has to be done over, the floors," she kicked at a loose tile, "the walls," she flipped off loose

15

coats of bluewash with one hand and pointed to several large cracks. "We spent a lot on this house, put in a bath with a linoleum floor and so on, but it's so big . . ."

Despairing of the house and wanting to cheer up the woman, I said, "Something smells good . . . like a delicious rice cooking."

"Aiee, *Madre de Dios*, the noodles!" she shrieked. "My noodles are burning! Pep! Pepito! Give the noodles a stir!" She scampered to the second floor with all of us trotting behind.

We kept up the same pace from then on, all nine of us running through the house at a giddy speed, the woman in the lead chattering without pause except for sudden bursts of laughter that infected us with fits of giggles we tried to smother. Sometimes one of us had to linger behind, doubled over in one of the cold, dark, peeling bluewashed rooms to regain control. The woman talked of the house, of wanting to sell it and be well out of it. She was not from the town, but from Barcelona, from the very center of the city, one of the busiest corners, not from some small lost-in-the-mountains pueblo where, God knows why, they had bought a house anyway and such a big one that there was no keeping it. We were on a terrace, bare and high walled, with a sparse glimpse of the mountains over the tops of the houses opposite, and a longer view of tiny vegetable gardens and fields stretching from the edge of town into the valley. The terrace was over the garage, she explained, an addition they had built. There was no car in the garage; perhaps that was another plan that fell through.

The kitchen had been left in its original state, a dark, almost airless space with the traditional charcoal grates for cooking set into a tiled shelf. The only thing that attracted us was the noodles, which smelled more and more delicious, bubbling in an earthenware pot with meat, tomatoes, onions, and red peppers. As the woman gave them a turn, we heard a hearty chuckle behind us. In a small room off the hall was her husband, a thin, wasted man with sunken cheekbones, colorless hair, and widely separated, yellowed teeth bared in a ghastly smile. He was sitting cross-legged on a chair, dressed in a two-piece suit of long winter underwear with a fur-collared black jacket slung over his shoulders. Gogol came to mind. He waved jovially at us, continuing to toast his stocking feet at the portable gas heater placed directly in front of his chair. At that moment, my husband came back from a tour of the now vacated master bedroom and solemnly handed me a photograph of a young man in a sailor's uniform with a handsome face, even features, a gentle serious smile, and dark liquid eyes.

"Her husband as a young man."

The shrunken old man in his underwear cackled in front of the gas burner.

"How handsome he was," I sighed.

"I was good-looking, too," the woman said. "We were both good-looking and rich. I inherited land worth four million pesetas, but my brothers took it. Aiee, the things that happen!" She began to wail and pace the room. To distract her, I asked if she had a picture of herself as a young girl.

"Here, here, it has to be in here," she replied, opening the drawer of a small table in the hallway. While the old man nodded and chuckled from his chair, she pulled out faded brown daguerreotypes and old photographs of large-boned, peasant-faced men and women and solemn, curly-haired little girls, all standing stiffly for the photographer in an artificial setting, next to an Oriental vase of flowers, in a garden swing set up in the photographer's studio. "That's my mother, the little girl that died would have been my sister, that's my grandmother . . ."

There were others, she said. Ignoring our protests, she dragged a rusty trunk into the hall and began passing

17

around photographs of nameless strangers who looked like all dead relatives of all Latin peasants. The floor was littered with faded flowers, old corset stays, and bits of yellowed lace, which the woman yanked, kneeling, from a trunk. Now that we were standing still, the cold of the thick, humid walls began to penetrate. We had to keep shuffling our feet to preserve some feeling in them.

Finally the smell of burning noodles rescued us. When the woman scurried to the kitchen with a cry, we turned as one to start down the stairs with exclamations of regret at having disturbed the dinner hour, interrupted her husband's sleep, and put her to so much trouble. She came back at a run. The ground floor! We hadn't seen the ground floor! The storeroom! The corral! Another time more convenient for her, on our next visit to the village, we called out as we hurried out into the welcome sunlight.

The couple in their cackling pathos stayed in our minds, but the impression made by the village was even stronger. Back in Paris, I pictured the cobbled streets with ruts worn deep by carts passing at sunrise and sunset every day for centuries, the fortress-walled houses, the welcoming, great arched door that opened wide to let in the cart or visitors, the sleepy square where old men sat in a row on stone benches next to a small Romanesque church, two straggling palm trees, and a flourishing fig. I remembered the friendly smiles and candid faces of the villagers. The setting haunted me, the views from every street onto hillsides so steeply terraced with stone walls that the slopes looked like one solid gray monument to man's struggle for bread, a struggle so desperate that he would plant even if there was room for only a single row of grapevines or a single line of almond trees. It was the human imprint that made the landscape warm and endearing, that gave a special charm to every roll and lilt of this mountainous northeastern corner of

Spain, the ancient, once independent province known as Catalonia. As someone aptly remarked: in Castile the landscape made the man; in Catalonia man made the landscape.

The following summer, again visiting Spain by car from Paris, we found ourselves near Las Casas del Torrente and went to visit it again. Señor Pedro was as cordial as ever, the weather far more clement, and our desire to leave modern city life for a tranquil village in the shadow of the past particularly keen. There were other houses for sale, Señor Pedro assured us, besides the one we had seen, which now stood vacant, abruptly abandoned by its unfortunate owners. A house would have to have a view, we said, a garden in back, and be sunlit in winter, but shaded in summer. There was such a house, he replied. It would have to have the original exposed wood beams, hand-painted tiles, and that indescribable something called character. That could be found too, he believed, and he was right.

The house was large. All Mediterranean peasant houses are, because there must be room to put away the cart and horse; to store the hay, olive oil, and tools; and to press, ferment, and store the wine. All these utilitarian rooms were on the ground floor, opening off a two-story entrance, overlooked by an interior kitchen window, up a flight of stairs to one side. The beauty, as in most Spanish peasant houses, lay in the proportions. Doors, windows, and walls were always precisely the right height and width, so perfectly combined and so natural that we felt at home in the house from the moment we entered. There was nothing to startle us, nothing we had to get used to or longed to change. The arched carriage door was large and inviting, the entrance scaled to match. From the street, you could see straight through the entrance, down the corridor, past the wine cellar and grain storage rooms to the walled plot in back and sunlit vineyards beyond. To the left of the entrance, an arch opened over a sloping passage for the cart to pass through. A stone well with hand-wrought iron pulleys stood on the other side, and beyond it was the horse's stall. The floors were covered with reddish-brown, handmade tiles, all of them scored by three fingers drawn across the wet clay to make deep indentations that kept the animals' hooves from slipping.

On the second floor, next to the kitchen, were more storerooms for dried tomatoes, strung decoratively across the room on ropes; for braided tails of garlic, hung from nails in the ceiling beams beside sausages and hams; for onions and potatoes spread out on the floor; and for sacks of dried white beans, lentils, chick-peas, and fava beans piled in one corner. A dining room, which also served as living room, sewing room, and workroom, was used for eating only when there were guests.

The kitchen, the center of the house, was the coziest, most inviting, and, to a foreigner, most interesting room, surprisingly like the kitchens unearthed at Pompeii and containing much the same equipment. An ancient Roman would have felt at home. He would have found the same fireplace in which most of the cooking is done, the same four-legged gridiron to put over the fire for broiling meat and fish, the same trivet to hold earthenware stewing pots, and the same chain and hook suspended over the middle of the hearth for the large iron caldron. He would have found frying pans, ladles, dippers, and stone or marble mortars shaped like those of Pompeii. As in Pompeii, he would be unable to bake at home except in the ashes of the fire, but he would use the village baker's oven, heated like ancient Roman ones by burning pine boughs, then raked clean before the baking begins.

Two walls of the kitchen were covered with blue and white hand-painted tiles. A braid of garlic strung on the wall and a six-gallon jar of olive oil stood ready for use. The triple sink was of hard yellowish stone. Below it was a pitcher for water and a straw-covered container of wine. Wine, I later learned, was often in greater supply than water, which had to be carried from a well a short distance from the village, though our house had both its own well and a cistern to collect rainwater from the tiled roof.

The upper floor of any peasant house had to have enough rooms to accommodate the three or four generations that usually slept there. It was therefore, like ours, always broken up into a series of small rooms. All the windows, upstairs and down, were tiny in order to keep out heat in summer and cold in winter, when the only warmth came from the kitchen fireplace and the sun. (Where the sun comes in, the doctor doesn't need to, the Catalans say.) Plumbing facilities were discreetly isolated at the far end of a long, narrow terrace lined with pots of flowers and clotheslines, it being the custom to put plumbing as far from the house as possible. I have heard that some laborers newly arrived in Barcelona indignantly refuse to move into apartments with inside bathrooms because they think them unsanitary.

Throughout the inside, and in front outside, the walls were whitewashed or bluewashed, while the back was bare mud and stone, blending almost indistinguishably with the landscape. The roof was constructed in the classical style of bare wood beams supporting cane mats, over which the red clay tiles were placed. We wondered about the roof. Standing on the third floor and looking up, we could see the sky through various openings. Señor Pedro, who again acted as our guide, told us not to worry. So long as we never repaired the roof, it would never leak. "They knew how to place tiles in the old days," he said, "but now you can never be sure. If you change the roof, it might run in buckets. But why don't you talk to the mason?"

It was then we met one of my favorite people in the

village, a man who spent a great deal of time in our house widening windows, enlarging rooms, drinking cognac, and talking of the past and the future. He came from a line of masons. His father, grandfather, and great-grandfather were masons, and perhaps his ancestors before that; memory did not go back farther. About seventy when I first met him, he was a lively man who walked pitched forward with a stumbling gait as if he were catching himself from falling at every step. Yet he could scamper over slippery roof tiles better than anyone around. "The roof is perfect, not one drop of water will come in," he declared after a quick trot across it, repeating what Señor Pedro had said. "Just don't ever touch it."

He went through the house, tapping on the beams— enormous trunks of wood reaching across the long, narrow rooms—examining the thick walls for cracks, and checking the floor tiles for dampness. There were just two dubious beams, to be replaced now or later on as we saw fit, he said. "But," he added as if he could not help himself, "why don't you build a new house? What do you want with an old one? You could build a nice modern house." It was hard to convince him we did not want a nice modern house, and it was at that moment that I had a premonition of the struggles I would have in getting him to make his repairs blend with the uneven masonry of the old house. "Now that it's badly done, do you like it better?" he used to ask me sadly after I had gotten him to make the sharp edge of a new wall uneven to match the old ones. "Don't tell anyone I did that," he would say, unhappily leaving the wall surface slightly bowed and bumpy instead of mirror-smooth.

Our walls joined the walls of other houses, one empty, the other occupied by two rabbits, three guinea pigs, and four chickens, all on the third floor, from which they peered through an open arcade at the mountains and valleys beyond. I later noticed that for some reason chickens were usually installed on the third floor, where they enjoyed the best view of all.

The house was everything we were looking for and the idea of living in a village appealed to us, but the actuality? For the moment we had quiet neighbors, but that could change. As residents rather than visitors, would we be resented? Invaded by overfriendly or overly curious neighbors? Would we find it dull? Too isolated? Barcelona was not far, some thirty miles away, but the narrow curving roads made it a forbidding drive. It was summer now, and country life as an alternative to city living was very attractive. Would it lose its appeal in the cold windy winter? The Mediterranean is a far colder place than anyone who has not lived there all year can imagine. We hesitated, then decided to rent for the summer to see. The owners, who had recently moved to Barcelona and returned to their house only for occasional summer weekends, were persuaded without much difficulty to rent it. Since it was equipped with all the household essentials, we moved in with only our suitcases and a feeling of adventure.

From the beginning, the villagers' smiles made us feel like welcome guests, and we, in turn, behaved like guests, making an effort to speak our hosts' language and respond in kind to their generous welcome. We smiled and waved at everyone we passed, offered a ride to anyone on the road when we drove, stopped often in the streets to talk when on foot, and took time when buying bread at the bakery or food in the shops to exchange a few words about the village, the weather, the crops, and the family. Soon we knew everyone in the village by sight if not by name. Everyone knew us from the first day, of course, for we were objects of curiosity at the beginning. Almost at once we heard them speaking of us as *simpatico*, rather as though we were not within earshot, the way people sometimes speak of children as if they were not there.

I was continuously surprised at how easily and willingly they accepted us and our ways, how open-minded and objective they were. I had imagined they might consider us lazy or resent us because our working hours were so much shorter than their long days in the fields. They gave the matter some thought, but the conclusion was not what I had expected. One day Paco, a peasant neighbor who eventually became one of our closest friends, remarked, "You may spend less time at it, but it's double work. We work many hours—all day long, but without having to think about it. Walking up and down the fields, you're free to think about anything you want, your mind can wander anywhere. Work in which your brain has to work and you have to be all present every moment is double work."

By the end of the summer, our car had become the unofficial ambulance of Las Casas del Torrente, having careened down the winding roads to deliver to the nearest hospital children with cuts or broken bones and women about to give birth. Once a week, on market day, the car was loaded with neighbors and baskets early in the morning and, at noon, it brought back live goats, chickens, ducks, and an enormous assortment of bundles and packages from Riera, the nearest market town, six miles away. The car, the neighbors warned us, ought to be put away somewhere to avoid its being damaged by curious or careless children playing in the street. Looking out an upper-story window of our house one day, we noticed the car was covered with spots; the windshield had what looked like white blotches on it, and the fenders were dotted with pink. "They were right," we thought, running out to have a closer look. To our delight we found the car not damaged, but decorated with flowers.

Whatever we did, we always felt too well rewarded by these charming, warm people; we were always in their debt. That first summer, our doorknocker frequently heralded a small child bringing a present of the first cherries, the first tomatoes, the first melons—or some newly laid eggs. Sometimes a live rabbit or goose thrashing wildly in a burlap bag was deposited shyly in our entrance. We shared picnics, expeditions, and feasts with our neighbors. Eventually we built true friendships on the mutual confidence established even that first summer, and came to enjoy a sense of belonging we had never had elsewhere.

Our summer experiment in renting was a success. By September we had decided to buy the house. By October we had decided to move into it permanently and close our apartment in Paris. We were becoming part of the village.

2

A Life

LARGELY SELF-SUFFICIENT, the village was a world in itself, and one foreign to me. I had known only cities, suburbs, and what pass for towns in America, those scattered conglomerations of shopping centers, central business districts, and houses isolated on yards, connected only by roads and cars. Here in Las Casas del Torrente, all the houses adjoined each other, sharing common walls, and everyone seemed to live in the street. Carts went up and down, mules were shod in the street, the baker unloaded his pine brush for fuel there. The women sat in their doorways working during the day and were replaced at night by their men, waiting for supper. Twice a day the goatherd passed with his flock, raising dust and the cries of women protecting the pots of carnations and geraniums lining their house walls. Children played in the street, dogs and cats slept and fought in the street, and people received each other in their doorways, bringing down a chair for anyone who stopped for more than a brief chat. If you wanted company or wanted to find out something, all you had to do was go out the front door into the street.

27

Much of what I learned about the village those first years came from talking to our neighbors the Solés who lived two houses down. I fell into the habit of stopping to chat with Grandfather Solé when I saw him sitting in the doorway, sometimes doing nothing, sometimes husking almonds, sorting dried vegetables, or repairing a harness. Grandfather Solé, or Señor José as he was called after Catalan custom, was the village cart maker as well as a farmer. Once in a long while I saw him working on a cart, repairing parts or replacing them, but I never saw him make a new one. "It's years since anybody ordered a new cart," he told me, his blue eyes crinkling in a smile. "Carts are finished now, but it doesn't matter, because I'm finished, too."

Since his heart attack two years earlier, he had stopped going to the fields and spent most of his time as all the old people did, sitting. When I came by, he would always offer me a chair, which his wife would bring down from the kitchen and I would accept, though I would have preferred to perch on the stone step. Like all the chairs in all the houses, it was cane-seated, ladder-backed, rigidly straight, and uncompromisingly uncomfortable. No villager, man or woman, had ever sat in anything with upholstery or arms or cushions, and there is nothing of the sort in their houses.

Even on a cold winter day, I would find Señor José in his doorway if the sun was out. The Mediterranean sun is so strong that you can be warm sitting in it when the temperature is close to freezing, so long as you are out of the wind. In summer Señor José sat in the shade just behind the doorway, where he could see everyone and everything that passed but stay out of the heat. Flies crawled over his face without his seeming to notice. Either he had acquired stoic indifference in years of working the fields despite heat, insects, fatigue, and rain, or else his deeply wrinkled, leathery skin was so toughened by exposure that he did not feel the flies. The furrows on his face looked like plowed fields, and his hands, resting on his cane, one over the other, were horny and spatula shaped, with black embedded in his squared, thickened nails. Yet his eyes were the surprisingly young, clear blue eyes of so many of the villagers, men and women, young and old, as clear and blue as the cloudless skies. Like all old village men, he wore dark blue cotton shirts and trousers, espadrilles tied on his feet, and a long, wide black cummerbund wrapped round and round his waist to serve as carryall and back support, and to keep the kidneys warm, winter and summer. All peasant men used to wear cummerbunds, still a common article in local shops, though most of the middle-aged and all of the young have changed to belts. Little by little, over a few years, I pieced together the story of his life.

He was born in 1899 in the same house in which he was to die, and in which his father and grandfather had been born and died. No one was born in hospitals in 1899, though the local doctor came to assist—and glad he was to have a job to do, Señor José told me. In those days, when people asked the doctor how things were, he used to shake his head morosely and complain, "There's a plague of health on these parts." Because for centuries only the strongest had survived childhood, through natural selection, a sturdy race had emerged, hard-working, hearty, and resistant. Of José's seven brothers and sisters, four died as infants, but the rest were never sick a day till they reached old age.

In José's childhood, life in the village was almost as it had been in medieval times except that the children had to go to school for a few years. If they learned much, they forgot it from lack of use. None of the old people I knew could do more than keep the simplest accounts, make change, and sign their names, all with fumbling and frowning. "Spain is years behind," José often said, shaking his

29

head. "We're ignorant . . . never learned anything. We know nothing of the world."

The known world of his childhood was a narrow strip reaching inland from Barcelona, a city many villagers never saw. There were no radios, no machines, no movies. No newspapers were read, no books owned. Men and women worked in the fields together, had seven or eight children, ate hugely at fiestas, sparsely at other times, and bought almost nothing with cash. *Chupetes,* the sweet young shoots that sprout on the grapevines in May, were the children's lollipops, and a pot of chocolate made a Sunday afternoon's entertainment for the women. Money was something to hide in a mattress against hard times, and there was little enough of it. For years, up to the Civil War, José worked as field hand for rich landowners who lived in Riera. They were good people, the Miros, he always said, ready to help anyone in trouble, generous, and honest. When the old woman died, people from miles around went to her funeral in genuine grief. And when the landowners raised his daily wage to two pesetas (the price of half a loaf of bread today), José worried that they would not be able to afford it.

When the café was built as a village cooperative, the villagers paid for it in labor and produce. The materials needed—mud and stone—were at hand in ample supply. To raise the little cash expended, every house gave the equivalent of two cartloads of wine and all of the once-pressed grapes that are sold to be pressed again and used in commercial alcohol. Everyone helped in the work.

José was just a child then, but he remembered clearly seeing it built, remembered how work was delayed when one of the only two carts in the village broke down, for carts were as rare then as cars were when we first came. Besides the carts, and before the carts, there were merely burros with saddlebags slung over their backs to haul the mountains of stones that went into the walls. Stones—they were more like boulders, those huge, uncut rocks a man could hardly budge alone.

The villagers must have had to manage without carts in building their houses, all of which were older than the café, though how they did it, I cannot imagine. When we put a new, rather small window in the front wall of our house, the hole cut out for the window left a pile of rocks waist high on either side. It took six cart trips to carry them off. There was no cement in that two-foot-thick wall, just rocks and fine, dry dust, once mud. "Have you ever seen a wall like that being built?" José asked us. We hadn't, of course. No new houses had gone up since we came. No new houses had gone up in José's lifetime or that of his father, for that matter, though José could tell us how the walls were built. The men haul up stones and balance one on top of the other so that the weight of the stones themselves holds them in place. Then they fill in the air spaces with mud, tramp it down with their feet, and start the next layer.

These stone and mud houses do not burn; the only wood is in the doors and exposed ceiling beams. The nearest fire truck is over twenty miles away, and no one has ever called for it. Since the one telephone in the village hardly ever works, trying to call would probably be pointless in any case. Fortunately, the only fires the village has known are chimney fires, put out by bucket brigades of neighbors on the roof. "It's slow building the old way, but we had time to build things that last for hundreds of years," José said, grimacing in disgust at the flimsy bricks walls slapped together in a day for the villagers' new chicken coops and pigsties. "We knew how to build in the old days, and we were as strong as the walls we made."

When his father took him out of school at age eleven, José went to work in the fields, too, but on Saturdays he walked six miles to Riera to learn the cart-making trade as

31

an unpaid apprentice. Whenever a neighbor roared by on a motorcycle while we were talking, Señor José would always shake his head in wonder and recall the miraculous day when, as a grown man, he bought a bicycle and was able to get to Riera in a quarter of an hour. "*Hombre,* I felt rich. Why, people talked as much in those days if a man got a bicycle as they do today if somebody goes and buys a car!"

Clocks were a rare luxury then, too. Even today, when there is a battered alarm in almost every house and a number of people have watches, the villagers seldom know the exact hour. If asked the time, a villager will reply that it must be about such and such because of the position of the sun, the work that has been done so far in the day, or because someone of fairly regular and known habits has passed by. The village mason stops for lunch when the shade of the church reaches a certain house. The baker complains that ever since his neighbor added a chicken coop on the roof, he can no longer judge the hour accurately by the shadow in the street. In his youth, José Solé woke up as his father had, getting up to stick his head out the window to tell by the position of the stars whether it was time to leave. He always left in the dark because he had to be in the fields two miles away by dawn. Every day till the light was gone, every day but Sunday, of course, he worked for the Miros. Sundays, he would work land of his own, all bought with money saved from wages and repairing carts, except for one vineyard his father had bought and planted for him. José told me of being taken on his tenth birthday to see the vineyard that was to be his.

"I planted this for you," his father said proudly.

"But why are the vines so crooked?" the son could not help asking. "Look how they zigzag!"

The older man was silent a moment before replying. "They are crooked, my son, because I planted them at night after I got through work, when it was too dark to see."

It was a hard life, José Solé was fond of saying, boasting of the work he had been able to do and of how he could go to a dance, dance all night, go straight to work the next day, and then do it all over again. "Still, it was a hard life, too hard," he would always conclude. "I wouldn't wish it on my son. I'm glad things have changed so he doesn't have to work like I did."

While the Solés had a few more possessions than in the past and a little more leisure, much seemed unchanged in my eyes. They had the same cart, mule, and primitive wooden plow, though José's son, Paco, now had a small motorcycle. They still spent little money on pleasure, though they spent more on artificial fertilizer, tools, and poisonous sprays. José Solé regretted every peseta spent. In his youth, when everyone wore homespun clothing and when trips to town were made only to sell at the market, no money was expended on clothes, amusements, housewares, or fresh meat and fish. All the household needed money for was salt herring, salt cod, and rice; church collections, First Communions, funerals, and marriages; occasional repairs, the shoeing of the mule, a few tools, and the village fiesta (for which each household was assessed), plus whatever pittance the man of the house might spend at the café or on tobacco. And that was all.

Even today the Solé family lived mainly on what they raised. Hay and carob beans were piled up for the animals, and wheat was delivered to the village bakery, where the baker's wife marked a blackboard with chalk to record how many sacks of wheat each peasant brought in and how many loaves of bread his family took out. In addition to their oil, wine, and stores of dried vegetables and fruits, the Solés had fresh vegetables all year. Although it might snow lightly once or twice, the vegetable garden provided salads, spinach, cabbage, cauliflower, and beets all winter. When I told Señor José of the snows covering the ground of the northern half of the United States from December through March, he remarked that it must be very hard on the vegetable plants. He was almost unable to believe there were none growing for so long a span, and he felt very sorry indeed for the inhabitants of such a bleak country.

José Solé's house was one of the few in the village in which a pig was still slaughtered at Christmas time to provide, after a feast of fresh meat, the sausages, hams, and bacon that hung from the ceiling of the storeroom, along with a fat, bladder-shaped, yellowed parchment full of white lard. Fresh pork meat was preserved in jars of olive oil, stored in the cool, dark ground-floor rooms. There were chickens, raised on table scraps and greens from the fields, a few hens for the family's eggs, and each May a tiny white kid was bought from the goatherd to be fattened until August, when it was killed for the *fiesta mayor,* the main holiday of the village. The young kid used to follow José Solé's wife around when she gathered greens in the fields for the animals. More than once, Señor José remarked that it was better behaved and more devoted than my dog. "And are you really going to eat it?" I would ask him. "So it seems," he would answer with a grin. "That's the way it is."

The Solés still worked for the same rich landowners, the Miros, but no longer as hired hands. Since the Civil War, they had worked on shares, two-thirds for themselves and one-third for the owner, with all the work done by, and all expenses paid by, the Solés. In addition, there were the fields the Solés owned, and two they rented. All in all, José cultivated more land than his father had, but the introduction of new methods and new products had lightened the labor and increased the yield.

"Those were Paco's ideas," José Solé said, "those new ways. I was against them, but some turned out all right. Now he keeps talking about a tractor, but it's too much money and we get along fine without it. Paco says if we don't get one, we can't go on. Well, he can get one when I'm gone if he wants to—I don't see it."

The changes had started just before the Civil War, he told me, and, of course, he talked of the war often, as anyone old enough to have known it did, always saying it was a thing that should never happen again, the most terrible, the most bitter of wars.

"We're hot-blooded," he said. "We've learned it's worth sacrificing many things to have peace because we don't play at revolt, we play for keeps."

There wasn't a house in the village that didn't lose a man or two. In the Solé household, the oldest son was killed fighting in 1938, when he was only eighteen. José had fought too; almost all men had, except the very old and very young. In Las Casas they had all been passionate Republicans—all, that is, except some of the newcomers to the village, outsiders from the south like Manuel, husband of the woman who did housework for us.

"War is stupid and doesn't get you anywhere," Manuel remarked one day. "Just take me, for instance. First the Republicans come, put a gun in my hands, and tell me to fight with them. Then the town where we are is overrun by Nationalists, who give me a gun and take me along to fight on their side. Does that make any sense?" He shrugged his shoulders. "I just went where I was told, managed never to fire a shot, and looked out for myself and the three dogs I had with me all through the war. If we found some milk, we'd drink it out of the same bowl, the three dogs and me, and at night they kept me warm. One," he patted with his hands to demonstrate, "one slept on my chest, one

35

on my stomach, and one by my feet. We came through all right, all four of us, but I never could see any sense to the whole thing."

For most of the villagers, war memories are bitter and tragic. Many were on the Ebro in that last desperate stand; many marched in pathetic lines to a dubious refuge in France. Hardly a child was born in the village for the seven years when most of the men were fighting or in exile, afraid to return home. The war left deep cleavages everywhere, but only once in a while was I made aware that the ground covering the holes is thin and the holes are deep. When the holes show through, Spaniards either hurriedly pass on to another subject or say firmly, "We have forgotten and buried that and we will not dig it up again." Indeed, though there was much talk of the war, it was seldom that anyone told his own story in detail. One day José Solé did, when his thirteen-year-old granddaughter Josefina was complaining that nothing ever happened in Las Casas. "It's better that it doesn't," said Grandmother Solé, knotting a thread. "You just don't know," José told his granddaughter, "you don't know what all happened." And he told his story while continuing to husk almonds for the coming winter.

There was such confusion and so many rumors when it started, so much talk of coups and plots and spies, that nobody knew what was happening except that, as José put it, "Franco was the revolutionary then and we were the government." For a while, though, nobody was certain who was the authority except that anyone who had a gun had authority. In the village nothing changed, but even as close by as Riera, the villagers did not know who was in charge anymore, though they had heard the mayor was no longer in office.

Soon after the rumors started, four soldiers came to Las Casas representing the government, three with machine guns and one without, but with a louder voice and more show of authority.

"He looked familiar to me," José said. "I was sure I had seen that red hair and large nose somewhere, and after a while, I recognized him as a clerk from the mayor's office. I don't know where he got the uniform and the authority because he was a fool nobody in his right mind would take seriously, but in those days stranger things happened."

The only person the four men came across in the street was José.

"There he was," José Solé's wife sighed, poking her crochet needle emphatically into the white shawl she was making, "the only one in the whole village out in the street. Why?"

José shrugged and continued. The clerk was strutting in his new role of being—who knows what, exactly? An authority anyway. The guns spoke for that. He asked José to point out the houses of all the landowners in Las Casas.

"I knew the Republicans were going around taking wine, oil, and wheat from rich houses for the front," José explained to us, "but there weren't any landowners living in Las Casas, and I told them there weren't."

The clerk kept insisting, and José kept insisting, until finally the clerk said, "Then take us to the house of the *sometente*." The *sometente* is the man in each village who has the right to carry arms in case of an emergency.

"I couldn't say I didn't know where the house was. With the clerk insisting and the three soldiers pointing their machine guns at me, what could I do? I took them to the *sometente*'s house and waited at the door. The wife came down, a big woman, hands on hips, angrily demanding what we wanted. I was on the spot because, of course, it looked like I was in league with them." José stopped to light a cigarette before continuing.

It was then the first shot of the war was fired in Las Casas. Only two of the soldiers had gone to the *sometente*'s house with José and the spokesman, while the third walked away in the direction of the church. As José turned toward the *sometente*'s house, a shot rang out. He found out later that the third soldier had blasted a hole right through the rose window, the pride of the village. "You can still see the scars," said José. "Everybody stayed in his house, quiet, with the doors shut. Everybody heard the shot, but nobody moved or looked out, and I didn't turn to look either."

"You see?" José's wife interrupted, looking to me for support. "Everyone in the village was in his house minding his own business but *him—he* had to be on the street."

The Las Casas priest was hiding like everyone else, more frightened than the rest because he'd heard the priest in the next town had been killed just a few days before.

"Why did they kill him?" I asked. "Was he a bad priest?"

"No," José answered, "he wasn't a bad priest, but when some men, Republicans, got up on a balcony in the main square and began making speeches, the priest got on his own balcony right across the street, shouting out how it was all lies and exaggerations. A day or two later, some men came for him, took him 300 yards outside the village, and shot him under an olive tree.

"Here in Las Casas, not so much happened. In towns and the bigger villages, there was more ugliness, more vengeance, more bad blood. People denounced each other just out of spite, and men got shot that way for nothing but a grudge. Our village was too small, we all knew each other too well for that to happen here."

The Las Casas priest, Father Casimiro, was in the sacristy when he heard the shot shatter the rose window. Terrified, he leaped out the back window and ran to the baker's house on the edge of the village, where he hid till nighttime. Disguised in the baker's stained old work clothes, he started running again at nightfall till he reached the lonely hermitage of San José, high in the hills above the village. There, the next morning, he came across the old man who guarded the place. The guard failed to recognize the priest in his dirty peasant clothes. Chatting about one thing and another, the old man said, "Did you hear how they shot the Reverend Father dead here?"

"Father Casimiro was so frightened when he heard the man say that," José recalled, chuckling, "that he took off over the hills. They tell how he was so scared that for every two bounds he took, he fell down on the third."

When he hadn't been heard from in a day or so, José, the baker, and a few other men became worried about Father Casimiro and set out to find him, driving across the mountains by cart in the dark, with the baker calling him to see if he would answer. They were sure the priest would know the baker's voice, but there was never a sound but the echo. They drove for miles, and though they questioned the priest in the second town up the road and felt that he knew where Father Casimiro was, they could find out nothing and had to turn back.

A few days later, new local committees were formed everywhere to run things, and the baker was elected head in Las Casas. Somehow the baker managed to get word to the priest, who, he had learned, was hiding in a cave in the fields, and he brought him food secretly every day until he could get him a pass to escape to Barcelona, where no one would bother to look for a poor parish priest. When the war was over, the baker was arrested and sentenced to death for having been one of the Republican leaders, but the priest came back, spoke for him, and got him off with three or four years in prison. Everyone agrees he was lucky. Men were shot for less or even by mistake, like one man from the village José told about who was so good, butter wouldn't melt in his mouth. He was taken away to prison, no one knows why, and when his wife went to visit him one day in the prison yard, she found him bleeding, shot dead, under a tree.

"Back there at the *sometente*'s house," José continued, "the clerk kept insisting the woman bring out all the guns and she kept insisting her husband had already turned them in, that there was only one weak hunting rifle that wouldn't do an army any good. Wait till my husband comes home for dinner, she pleaded, he'll tell you. The fool of a clerk said she was lying, pushed her aside, walked in, and started to search a little room off the entrance. I felt embarrassed standing there while he emptied out a chest of drawers, with two armed men standing by. All he pulled out was old clothes, corks of all sizes, and broken tools. At last, I had to speak up, not to the clerk, because he was such an idiot, but to the soldiers.

"'Aren't you afraid of looking foolish?' I asked. 'When you come into a village, you're supposed to go to the leaders, tell them your orders, and get them to help. Instead, here you are rifling through the drawers of a citizen and scattering corks and old clothes on the floor for no reason.'

"One of them turned to the other and said, 'Maybe we *are* making fools of ourselves. What are we doing here anyway?' The other nodded, and both stood a moment in confusion. In the meantime, the clerk had moved on to a second chest that had one drawer open, lined with straw, and filled with a litter of puppies so young they didn't have their eyes open yet. 'That looks like a likely hiding place,' the clerk said as he seized the drawer with the puppies in it, but just as he touched it, in came the bitch, a large, white dog moving like white lightning, so fast it had its teeth in the fool's trousers before anyone could make out what it was. It looked like a white ghost of vengeance. The fool was howling, the woman was shrieking and pulling at the dog, the dog was yelping, and the soldiers with their machine guns were turning as red as the clerk's hair. As soon as the woman got hold of the dog, the three of them left without a word and never came back.

"I felt like laughing, it was so ridiculous, but it's sad, too, to see authorities behaving that way. How can you have any respect after such goings-on?"

The confusion continued. New committees were formed, new men came to requisition oil, wine, blankets, and wheat for the front from the houses of landowners, or "proprietors" as they were called in the jargon of the Popular Front. No one dared oppose men acting on government orders, but José said it was sometimes so ridiculous he felt ashamed just talking about it. "Proprietors indeed!" he said. "The sister of one of them was in Riera learning to be a hairdresser, that's the kind of proprietors they were!" After the war, members of the village committee had to pay out of their own pockets for everything that had been requisitioned. It was the old government that had made the requisitions, but it was the committee that paid.

"Such ridiculous things happened, you could hardly believe it," José continued, shaking his head. "Like one time . . . I was on the front, the Ebro. There was very little food then. I got enough because I worked in the mess hall, but I'd otherwise have been half starved like the rest. Well, one day when I was sent out with another soldier to find food for the mess hall, we came across a farmhouse where the woman still had some rabbits. Agreeing on a price was no problem because there was plenty of money then, just nothing to buy. The woman handed over all but one rabbit for the price agreed on, and then the soldier demanded the last rabbit, which was a female, already carrying a litter. 'What do you mean by holding out on me?' he snapped. 'Hand over that rabbit!' When he insisted, I stepped in. 'Let her keep one rabbit, what's the difference?' I said. 'In a month or so, she'll have more rabbits to eat. It's stupid to kill the future.' He whirled around, poking his gun in my face. 'What are you doing?' he snarled. 'Are you defending a proprietor?' A proprietor! Of one rabbit! It makes you ashamed.

"And then the Ebro—there was no need to kill so many men for nothing. There was no hope. Why keep fighting just to get killed? I don't see how the authorities could have allowed it . . . We were beaten. And then we took off, for France."

Barcelona fell on January 26, 1939. Within ten days, France officially opened her borders to the half-million refugees who streamed across the frontier with no papers, no food, no money, no home, and no future. The world hailed the French government's generosity.

"France," sighed José. "The French despised us, and the longer I stayed, the worse things got." After World War II broke out, there was not enough food to go around, yet the hungry hordes of wretched refugees were there to stay. Herded into camps, able-bodied Spaniards like José were assigned to work gangs in fields or factories and kept virtually prisoners, allowed to go only a short distance from the enclosures. *"Mierda de español*, always making trouble," the French official said to José when he asked for a pass to go get shoes for the winter.

The Spaniards were moved north and south in France, always under guard and under suspicion. José told of an incident when his work gang was being transferred from one train to another somewhere in central France. French soldiers guarded the Spaniards, who passed down the crowded railroad platform in single file, but despite the guards a man in front of José managed to snatch the suitcase of a French priest waiting on the platform and conceal it in a heap of shabby refugee bundles. José waited a moment, hoping the soldiers had noticed; then, without a thought for the vengeance that might fall on him when he was alone with his fellow Spaniards in camp, he reported the man to the French guards. "I couldn't let that Spaniard rob a priest," he said, "because it touched the honor of all of us."

All the Spanish refugees had reason to believe they were on the Nationalists' blacklist and in danger of prison or death should they return to Spain. Nevertheless, when the Germans, desperately short of manpower as events turned against them, began taking Spaniards off for forced labor at factories and camps under heavy Allied bombing attack, José, like many others, decided to risk going back.

"Sure it was dangerous," José said, "but things weren't going to get any better where I was. I was fed up, you know, and desperate, and I hadn't heard from my wife and family all this time, so I decided to risk it. I was planning to go with another Catalan, but he got a pass on some trumped-up excuse while I didn't so he went on. That same night, I took off anyway, pass or no pass, alone, planning to travel only in the dark because I had nothing to show if I was stopped. I'd hide if a car went by, which wasn't often. Then I was lucky enough to see a truck parked at the side of the road, headed south like me. The driver was up front, cursing, trying to get the motor started. I sneaked up from the back, hid under some sacks, and sure enough, the truck went the right way and got me over a hundred miles south before it slowed up to turn and I jumped out and rolled into a ditch. The driver never saw me, but I've never forgotten him, because I had a long way to go and my shoes were already falling apart."

The way José went, which was the route many others took, led along the Pyrenees into the interior, where there were no soldiers to be seen, few inhabitants, and the rugged frontier was impossible to guard. Occasionally José asked his way of a Catalan-speaking shepherd. Walking thirty miles a day through snowfields, over windswept passes, through the prickly underbrush of high plateaus, where only

43

goats and wild boar passed, he reached Spain without being challenged. For two weeks he walked, sleeping in the open or in a farmer's barn. It was risky to ask for food and shelter, but it was good to get in out of the rain. Once it turned out that the farmer was organizing a wild boar hunt for the local authorities and was able to warn José not to continue the way he'd planned because he would have ended up right in the middle of the hunt. In another place, a farmer advised him to walk straight down the railroad tracks the way everybody else did because he'd look suspicious going through the thick of the mountains.

"I felt I stood out like a lone pine tree there in the open, but no one stopped me, and once I got to Barcelona, nobody was likely to as long as I stayed out of trouble.

"First thing I did in Barcelona was look up a cousin of mine. It happened he'd lost his wife and had four children on his hands, but he took me in. To help him out, I started cooking for him. I'd learned something about making food go farther in the mess hall, and he didn't want me to leave because he said they were all eating better and more on the same rations since I came. But after I'd been there a few weeks, half hiding in the apartment all day, I told him it was no good for either of us, that I was no housewife. I had to get out, get a job, and earn some money.

"In the meantime, I'd found out about my family, that my wife and two youngest sons were fine, but my oldest had been killed fighting. I also found out I was suspected of being responsible for the death of the oldest son in the *sometente*'s house, the house I'd had to go to with the men with machine guns. It wasn't true . . . Fact is, I hadn't even known he was dead. Still, there were plenty of men with no blood on their hands who got shot just the same, and it didn't look safe to go back yet.

"Through another relative I got a job delivering vegetables from truck gardens around Barcelona to the central market with a cart and burro. The only trouble was, I couldn't do it. If you're used to it, you can manage—the other fellows did. The man who unloaded with me got all the sleep he needed right there on top of the cart. He'd start snoring as soon as he climbed on top of the cabbages, but I had to drive the cart. The other drivers, the ones who were used to it, had a technique for sleeping. They'd put the cart wheels on the railroad tracks, and the cart would go right along in a straight line. The burros used to sleep, too, walking on the tracks. Everyone slept going to Barcelona that way. There weren't many trains then, only about one every half hour, and when one came, the driver would wake up right away, get the cart off, and then get it back on, and everyone would go back to sleep; but you had to know how to do it. I didn't learn fast enough to last. After three months I quit, half dead, and decided to come back to Las Casas.

"I was warned it wasn't really safe yet, though. Those days you could never be sure. So when I came back, I hid in a cave all day, going out at night when it was dark to work the fields, then going back into hiding. Of course, everyone in the village knew I was back because they saw my fields were worked, though they never saw anybody in them in the daytime. No one said anything, not a word. And no one saw me. I wasn't the only one—another man came back and hid in his own house without any of the neighbors seeing him for six months. But when everyone could see his wife was with child, everyone knew he was back, so he came out of hiding . . . and nothing happened. When I heard that, I just went to work the fields in daylight one day and everyone acted as if I'd been there all the time and it was the most natural thing in the world. Nothing happened, then or ever, but if I'd come back right away, I might have been taken out and shot on the spot."

"I don't know why you had to get mixed up in it," his

wife interjected again. "That's what got you in trouble. *You* were the one to show them the *sometente*'s house, *you* were there when they requisitioned things for the front, *you* rushed off to join the army—"

José smiled. "Yes," he said, "when things happen, a man has to act . . . and take the consequences."

The village returned slowly to normal, the dead were mourned, the last exile came home, the baker was released, and Franco earned everyone's gratitude for keeping strife-weary Spain out of World War II. The decades of peace began. Republicans like José, along with anarchists and communists, put aside their politics with their guns. There were fewer men to work the land in Las Casas. In previous generations younger sons usually ended in Barcelona because there wasn't enough work on the land for all. "How many grandfathers there are in Barcelona!" José's daughter-in-law, Sara, once remarked, but that came to an end with the war. Paco, José's youngest son, had been sent to Barcelona to work in the café of a distant relative but was called back in 1946, when his brother was killed in a fall into an abandoned well.

Although men were scarcer, the means at their disposal were greater. José and Paco could do what four men had done before and get better results. Still, José was reluctant to give modern methods their due. "It's all the same," he would say. "Look, we've been turning the soil over between rains for hundreds of years because we know it makes plants grow better. Now Paco, who reads all those magazines and listens to government talks on the radio—he tells me the reason we do it is to get rid of air pockets that would dry out the soil. Knowing that doesn't make any difference, does it? You do the same thing you did before anyway."

By the end of the 1950's, Spain's growing prosperity had begun to reach villages like Las Casas, but José Solé, by then an old man, saw change and prosperity through mists of reminiscence, illuminated by the brighter joys of his youth. If I remarked that the farmer seemed to live better than he had a generation ago, José would deny it. I used to search for concrete examples he would be unable to dismiss, but I never won the argument. What about electricity? I asked one day.

"That's new, all right," he said. "I remember when it was put in in 1930. But we saw just as well before with the petroleum lamps we used to have. If my father had to write a letter, he'd set a lamp right in front of himself and write perfectly well. These days, if a bulb burns out on the street, you stub your toe on a stone at night. There was no such problem before. You knew the street in the dark and never stubbed your toe."

When television aerials began to sprout from rooftops after we had been in the village just two years, I pointed to them as a sign of prosperity. The old man shook his head. "For one thing, you don't have to have money to buy things nowadays, so anybody can afford anything. In the old days, nobody bought anything, whether he had money or not. It's just a change of habit . . . people used to save, now they spend. Take Antonio Gorri, now. You'd never think he was rich, would you?" He was a poorly dressed old man, always hard at work. "Well, he probably has more money stashed away in a sock than you or I could count, but you can bet he counts it. That's his pleasure, counting money."

"Every man has his own way of enjoying himself," Grandmother Solé remarked. "Some like to go fishing, some like to make money."

"He's not a bad sort," José went on. "You can talk to him. But he has that one vice. Like Malla, now. He's rich. He owns a big house in Riera, a lot of land here and miles away from here, too. They say he even owns an apartment house on the beach that he rents at high prices to foreigners

47

in summer. And he's so shrewd, he can feel a peseta in the air when no one else can and grab it before your eyes." José illustrated with a swift gesture as if catching a fly in midair. "Yet he works like any poor peasant, alone and hard, more than any of us, because he works every day of the week, every moment he can, even in the dark. We smile and turn over in bed when we hear his tractor before dawn, and we can still hear it after dark when we have supper in the evening. And with all that, he never spends anything if he can help it. To save, he drinks water instead of wine and sleeps out in a hut in the fields on a sack to save the gas he'd use driving home."

"And to be ready to work earlier in the morning," put in Grandmother Solé with a chuckle. "You live as if you were never going to die, I told him one day. Do you think you can take it with you? All that money you've stored up, you'll never see again, but your heirs will be enjoying it as you never did . . . Old Malla just laughed and turned back to his plow."

"There're still a few like him," José said, "but nowadays people are more apt to spend money than hoard it, and they spend on different things. In the old days, when we had a village fiesta, we used to set up a huge tent there in the main square and hire two orchestras, the best there was. People would come from miles around to eat and drink and dance for three days. That was our television. Whether you spend for one thing or for another . . . it all comes to the same!"

Then he started talking in the way of old men about the keener pleasures of the old days and, as is the way with such talk, I never knew how much was true and how much was colored by memory. Because if it was true, it is better to eat salt herring, sardines, boiled vegetables, lentils, and chick-peas, and little of that, even on Sundays, so that come

Christmas and Easter and the village fiesta, you can feast on chickens, rabbits, and kid for days with gusto and remember it for weeks or months.

"I remember going to the fields for forty days with just a tiny piece of bread and forty figs during Lent," said José. "When we came home at night, we'd sit around the fire telling the rosary, then have a supper of herring, cabbage, and potatoes, and go to bed. For forty days. You can imagine how much we looked forward to Easter! Now when it comes, nobody even wants all that food and meat because we have it all the time!"

I thought I might win the argument at last.

"From what you say, the farmer eats better now than he used to," I ventured. "Now there's one thing that's certainly improved."

"Well, maybe," Señor José drawled, "yet . . . I don't know. More meat more often, yes, but it's not good anymore. The chickens we fed scraps and greens for six or eight months . . . those were chickens! Now you can fatten a bird up in three months by pumping it full of fish meal, but what does it taste like? Give me a good piece of salt cod and greens any time."

His wife had just come in from the corral where she had been feeding the kid goat, which tried to follow her out into the entrance, nuzzling her skirts.

"Nothing tastes the way it used to," she chimed in. "Take eggs, now. We still keep a few hens on grain, but there's hardly a house in the village where they don't give them at least some store feed. Here," she said, holding out some of the eggs tied in her apron. "Try some of these. You've probably never eaten *real* eggs."

"I wonder if you'll see the difference," Grandfather Solé said. "It's harder to recognize the good if you're used to bad than the other way around."

49

As Grandmother Solé wrapped the eggs in a tiny scrap of paper, her husband told her to get another piece to wrap up some of the chick-peas he had been sorting.

"She doesn't like those," Grandmother Solé said.

"Said she did," he replied as she handed him a page from an agricultural magazine.

"I guess nobody likes chick-peas much around here," he explained as he skillfully wrapped up several handfuls in the single sheet of paper, "because we ate almost nothing else during the war. However, all food is good food. In fact, some foods people think aren't so good really are, if they'd just open their minds to it. For instance, one late afternoon a couple of years ago, I was coming home from market in Riera in the cart. It was November, so it was dark out already, but I could see something ahead of me get hit by a car and tossed on the side of the road. As I passed, I saw it wasn't a dog as I'd thought at first, but a hare, a big handsome one that must have weighed a good twelve pounds. I picked it up, still warm, just killed by a blow from the car that minute, so I took it home. Well, when my family heard I'd picked it up on the road, they wouldn't have any part of it. None of my neighbors would either, though anyone could see it was perfectly fresh and killed cleaner than if it had been full of gunshot. But there you are . . . I ate it by myself and had to give the rest to the dog because no one would have it."

"Of course not. It was disgusting," said his wife.

"It's all in your head, woman," he answered as Grandmother Solé went upstairs to start cooking the midmorning meal, or *almuerzo*, and the rich smell of potatoes and onions frying in olive oil came down to us. "Now take cat for example," José continued, addressing me while picking up in one hand a playful kitten at his feet and gesticulating in the air with it. "You ever eaten cat meat?"

"No. That is, not that I know of, though I've heard it's hard to tell cat from rabbit when it's cooked."

"Some people ask to see the head when they eat rabbit in restaurants," he said, "or else the ears. But there's another way you can tell."

"How?"

"By the bones. Cat bones come out smooth and clean when you eat. Rabbit bones don't. But I, for one, can say it's just a prejudice about cats." He gave the kitten a toss. It landed lightly three or four feet away and scampered off. "If people didn't know what they were eating, they'd find it perfectly good."

"Did you ever eat a cat yourself?" I asked.

"I did," he said, "and a very large cat it was. It took me some time to go about it though," he added, settling more comfortably as he started to tell the story. Here, where people have time, few distractions, and no books, story-telling is a common pastime. One evening when several of us were sitting around the kitchen fire, a man began telling a tale which, to my surprise, turned out to be the story of Christopher Columbus, with many details I had forgotten or never known.

"We had this big fat cat some years ago," Señor José began, "twice the size of a normal cat and a stubborn, sly animal. It kept the mice and rats out all right, but we found a rabbit missing from the corral one day. Another day, another rabbit was gone, and a few days later, another one. We'd been saving them for the fiesta, and we weren't going to have much of a feast if that continued. There was more stealing in those days, more poor people. There were more foxes, too. Still, there just seemed no way a person or an animal could have got in. Anyway, I decided to wait up all night to catch whoever or whatever was stealing rabbits. I sat there in the dark alone, hidden in the shadows, waiting and getting more and more scared thinking what I would do if it was a person after all. Then I saw it happen. The cat came along a ledge, stalking and crouching. Like a panther, it lit on a rabbit and carried it off, dead, killed with one stroke. I took after the cat with a stick of wood in my hand, but it not only got away—it made off with the rabbit, too.

"The next day at breakfast, I told my family it was the cat, and that since the cat had eaten the rabbits, I was going to eat the cat. Which was only right." He looked at me expectantly and I nodded. "The cat must have heard me because from that time on, I could never get near it. It was very affectionate with the rest of the family, almost like a dog, but never came within arm's length of me from that day.

"I don't know if my family believed me, but all I was waiting for was rain, and every time I saw the cat, I said, 'Next rainy day, I'm going to take that cat and cook it and eat it.'"

I nodded again. I had learned by then that a peasant can't work the land on rainy days, so he has time to do other things, or to do nothing at all.

"One morning I went off to the fields as usual, but about eleven in the morning it started to drizzle. I could see it was going to rain on and off all day long. I headed back home thinking about the cat. It was a very smart cat because when I came in the house, I didn't see it anywhere though I looked all around. My family wouldn't tell me a thing, but when I went to change my wet shoes, there it was in the closet with its eyes shining like brass buttons. I downed it with a flying tackle, stuffed it in a sack, with it all the time going *pffft-pffft-pffft* so loud it sounded like a steam engine, and I killed it, skinned it, put a large pot on the stove, and told my family to get ready to eat a stew such as they never ate before.

"Well," he paused, shaking his head, "they would have none of it. Said they didn't want to see me or the cat in the house. Since it had stopped raining for the moment, I took the cat and the pot out to the fields, where I fried up some onions and tomatoes in oil and added some peppers and potatoes and the cat. Seeing as the rest of them wouldn't touch it, I ate the whole thing myself. And I can tell you, that cat was good. Best cat we ever had."

"Savages, brutes. Ay, *los hombres*," clucked Sara, coming down the steps from the kitchen, her full, long skirts swinging from side to side, a straw basket covered with a napkin over one arm. "This is better than cat any day," she said, drawing back the napkin to show me a thick, well-browned potato omelet on a plate, an enormous chunk of crusty bread, some olives, tomatoes, and onions for a salad, a few pieces of fried fish, and a flask of white wine.

"I'm just taking it to the fields for Paco's *almuerzo*," she said. "Want to come along for the walk?" I nodded. It was just ten o'clock and a fine sunny morning. José Solé wished us a good journey as if we were going to the end of the earth, and we started down a dusty road little wider than a cart track, leading through groves of olive, almond, and carob trees, and acres of vineyard, where the grapes hung, glistening, fat, and waiting.

3 ❧

Harvest

THE ROAD reflected the white quiet of morning. The earth
was still cool in the shade of the vine leaves, but the green
grapes were drinking the hot sun greedily, turning it to
sugar, and the air, refreshed from the night, was warming like a slow oven. The chirping and whirring of sparrows
and swallows around the house and the monotonous cuckoo
of the crested *poopoot* in the fields gradually diminished
as the sun climbed. Just as the heat and stillness reached
a peak, the *marinada*, or sea breeze, sent a cool relief over
the village, ruffling the vines and stirring the fine, sandlike
dust of the streets. The scent of the sea, thirty miles away,
blended with the smell of hot earth, green leaves, and pine-
covered hills overgrown with rosemary and thyme.

There is a saying that the Catalans make bread out of
stones. Looking at the landscape, I felt it was true. Stones,
often worn deeply by thousands, millions, of cart wheels,
jutted up in the dirt road; stone walls lined the roadside,
divided every patch and held it in place on the hills; stones
lined the cisterns dug in the ground to catch rainwater—
all of them stones taken from fields that were still filled

with stones. If you removed them all, perhaps there would be no foothills left, I thought, but where would you put them? The peasants had done what they could with them. Their houses, their walls, and the curious igloo-shaped round huts they built in the fields for tool storage and shelter were all made of stones, piled one on top of the other without cement.

"Is it far?" I asked Sara idly, not caring.

"To the bottom of the hill, across the *torrente*, and up over the top. It's not far, though we have fields closer, too . . . and farther away. One of them lies beyond that mountain. You can see the sea from there on a clear day."

The distant pine ridge she pointed to was at the end of the valley.

"How can you take care of it that far away?" I wondered.

"When we go, we set out in the cart before dawn, about two or three in the morning, so we're there by the time we can see, and head back only when we can't see anymore. But since we have just olive trees there, we only have to go a few times a year."

I asked where their other fields were. Only one small field of olives was near the house. Other patches of land lay scattered in the valley, about a mile away, some north, some south; another was on the way to the olive grove across the mountain. Because most of the fields were out of sight, the Solés had to anticipate when it was necessary to attend to each and what it would need at that moment. Without any written records, José Solé directed the routine, seeing that everything was tended in turn and in time, the vegetable patch, the melon fields, the vineyards, olive groves, almonds, the carob trees that provided food for the animals, and the wheat fields.

We crossed the dry wide bed of the canyon so gloriously dubbed "El Torrente," where a flock of black goats was grazing under the watchful eyes of the village goatherd and his motley, intelligent dogs. When I first arrived in the village, I had been told El Torrente supplied the water for Riera and its expanding suburbs, for all the fields along its bed, for the village cisterns in rainless seasons, and for the local laundry vats. When I went down to have a look at it, expecting a rushing torrent, I found not a trace of water. If that was the source we were to rely on, the future looked pretty dry, I thought. "There's plenty of water in it," Sara assured me, "but it's all gone deep underground. You can still see water in it sometimes, more than you'd ever believe. When there's a big storm and the mountain snow melts and rushes south, a flash flood can fill it up in the moment it takes to cross it!"

The villagers tell about a man crossing one day with his cart, the *torrente* being just as dry as I had always seen it, when suddenly the sky opened up and the floodwaters came down to fill the riverbed in one terrifying rush. Cart and mule were swept away, never to be seen again, though the man somehow caught onto a rock and managed to save himself.

Water fascinates Spaniards, for the land of the olive is the land of the almost rainless summer. The famous Arabic pools and fountains of southern Spain could only have been designed by people from a dry country. If you put a Catalan peasant in front of Niagara Falls, I don't think he would be able to believe what he saw. And while Sara may say there is plenty of water in El Torrente, it would be considered a sin to use any more of it than absolutely necessary, which, for a Catalan, is very little indeed. Two gallons a day are enough for a family of four without a vegetable garden or animals. When I told my neighbors that an American family of the same size uses 200 gallons per day, they could not imagine how it was possible. Paco, after giving it some thought, concluded that Americans

57

must turn on the tap when they get up in the morning and never turn it off.

When it rains in Catalonia, the storms are often terrifying. You think the houses are going to slide loose and slip down into the valley, the way the water sweeps past. The earth washes away until the dirt streets are an impassable jumble of stones. Some storms last seven or eight hours, with cracks of thunder loud enough to split the sky every few seconds and an intermittent flaring of light that resembles nothing so much as amateurish stage effects, interrupted by bolts so bright they hurt the eyes. Sometimes balls of fire hurtle across the sky. Sara's aunt, Tía María, goes out in the storm to command the lightning by striking one rock on another in a secret formula taught her by her mother. No one is allowed to watch her, and no one knows the formula. Because she has no daughter, the formula will be lost, and we will have to get a lightning rod.

"Do you really believe Tía María can keep lightning away?" I asked Sara.

"I don't know," she answered, smiling. "There are things we don't understand. I just wish she could keep rains away, too. If we get them right before the harvest, it can ruin us. The mud gets so thick in the fields, the carts can't get in, and the grapes rot on the vines before we can pick them." Then she added the peasant's favorite philosophical phrase. "But what can you do? That's the way it is. If God wills, we'll have a good harvest this year."

The vineyard we were passing was heavy with fruit, clear-skinned, translucent pellets, unblemished by mildew or the thousand other plagues that can injure or destroy a crop almost overnight. Of the Solés' lands, the vineyards were the most important, the most extensive, and provided almost all the family income except for a little money from the sale of olive oil and melons. In the years when the blossoms did not freeze in a late snow, the Solés harvested a fair quantity of almonds, but no one in Las Casas ever counted on almonds for income. The climate was too undependable. Like vegetables, almonds were grown mainly for household use.

Looking back down toward the *torrente*, we waved at the women gathered at the village laundry, a collection of large vats of water under shade trees. Laughter and voices wafted up to us.

"There's talk of putting running water in the village, like in Riera," Sara said, "but the women don't like the idea."

"When they have to carry the clothes on their heads half a mile and back and keep running to the village well all day? I should think they'd be clamoring for running water!"

"They *like* going to the well and the laundry," Sara replied. "They say otherwise they'd never have a chance to get together and talk."

Just over the hill, we saw Sara's husband, Paco, tying his mule under a fig tree and putting on its feedbag. He waved with a broad smile. "I knew you'd come along just now. So did the mule. He went down the last row and stopped right in the shade."

We felt cool at once under the tree. I don't know if it could be proved, but the temperature seems to drop several degrees under a fig tree, and the peasants all insist that it does. Sara and I munched a few olives and drank wine from the spouted glass flask known as a *porrón* from which all Catalans drink, holding it high in the air and, with tilted head, swallowing the jet of wine. Paco ate with the same pleasure and complete dedication to the task that he showed in everything he did. If the government ever wanted to promote farming, Paco would make a perfect poster peasant. At thirty-four, he was at the peak of his powers, radiating health, strength, and joy, and you had only to see the fields he worked and compare them with neighboring fields to know he was the best farmer around.

"That was good," Paco said, finishing his hunk of bread. "Some days the baker really makes good bread like in the old days."

"Except it never keeps the way it used to . . . dries up in a day," his wife put in.

The old days, the old days, I kept hearing the same refrain. Had we come too late even to this remote village to live in the past? And if it had changed so, was life better or not for the villagers? I asked Paco and Sara, adding that I had just had a long talk with Paco's father about it.

"It's much better now," Paco answered, and Sara nodded agreement. "I wish our grandfathers could come back just to see the way we live compared with twenty years ago. They wouldn't believe it. There was more misery before, lots of beggars, and people were poor, really poor. Now you can even afford a luxury. For instance, if you wanted to, you could go to Valencia, just for the trip. Maybe you'd give up something else to do it, but you could go."

In the old days, money was for saving, produce for storing, and daylight hours for working. The habit of saving was still strong. The accounts I paid at the village stores were added up on the smallest piece of paper the figures would fit on, something the size of two thumbs, and when the doctor came to our neighbors' houses at night, a child would be sent to borrow a light bulb from us to replace the fifteen-watt bulb that was the strongest they had.

"We used to save every scrap we could," Sara said. "If we had a little salt cod for breakfast, we saved the skin to flavor the noon rice, along with a bit of bacon rind. Even bread was scarce, though it was good bread, I must say, and baked fresh every day."

"Your father seemed to think life was better before," I commented to Paco.

"He's getting old," Paco answered. "He doesn't remember."

"I remember," Sara said, "I remember his sister telling me once how one lamb chop did for all the children. There were four of them. First she ate the fat around the outside, then the oldest boy ate the meat around that, the middle one ate the round center piece, and the last gnawed the bone."

"We work much less now, too," Paco put in.

In the days when José Solé used to set out at three in the morning and come back at ten at night, he had little to show for it. There wasn't even enough olive oil for the household, Paco recalled, though olive oil is as basic as wine. It replaces butter on bread and in cooking, cures a hundred ills from a rash to an earache, lubricates squeaking doors and rusty tools, waxes floors, and preserves wood, among other things. The trees yielded so little, the Solé household used to have to buy oil, and the children were admonished to put only a dribble on a piece of bread. "Not so much! Not so much! I remember mother telling us," Paco said. "We still have the same old olive trees, but they give us plenty of oil for the house and plenty left over to sell, too, because we can feed them now. I remember helping in the fields as a little boy, putting fertilizer on the vines. If there was a vine near an olive tree, father would always say, 'Don't put any on that one or the olives will eat it all up.' So the olives had to live on what was in the land, which wasn't much, poor things." He crumbled a handful of the dry, red pebbly dust in his calloused palm. "We get three times as much from the same land today and with less work. Still," he added thoughtfully, lighting a cigarette and leaning back against the fig tree, "we'll have to change a

61

lot more, and quick, if we're going to make a living from it."

I was puzzled. He had just said everyone was making a better living.

"Yes," Paco agreed, "but you see, the fertilizer and the sprays against diseases you have to put on today all cost much more, and the wages you have to pay harvesters are higher and higher, but the prices you sell at aren't going up much. The farmer, especially the small farmer with poor land, is being squeezed out." He brought the palms of his hands together slowly to illustrate. "You can barely make a living off land alone anymore. You have to put in animals, chickens, or pigs or something, and even then . . . the baker's tried one thing after another and nothing seems to work. You have to get machinery, modernize, have a tractor."

"Is that what you're going to do?" I asked.

"Right now, it's pretty hard to," Paco said slowly. "The old people don't understand; these changes have come too fast. Father's gone along some. All this fertilizing and spraying, for instance—he was set against it at first. But whenever I got him to try it, he saw for himself that it worked and that spending pesetas brought in more pesetas. It was a whole new idea, spending to earn, a break with the old routine ways. It's funny, you know—it used to be the father who showed the son what to do. Now it's the other way around. Still, the father rules in the end. What can we do? That's the way it is. It's all come too fast."

"We have to be patient," Sara put in. "How do we know what we'll be like when we're old? It isn't easy."

"I can't hold out much longer this way," Paco said, frowning. "A farmer has to mechanize today or he's finished."

"If you had a tractor, wouldn't you miss your mule?" I asked, thinking of the long day alone in the fields. "Doesn't he keep you company?"

"Of course, poor beast. He works when I work, he eats

when I eat, he rests when I rest. It's company, all right. He knows when it's time to go home, too, and jogs down the last row faster and happier, knowing, like me. But he eats, the wretch. Now you take a tractor—when it's not working, it doesn't eat." He chuckled and added, "That reminds me of a story," and he told an old story about a peasant in the village who kept complaining about how much his mule ate. One day, a neighbor jokingly suggested a very simple solution: if he stopped feeding the mule, it wouldn't eat. The owner of the mule began calculating how much he would save and decided it was a good plan. The first day he skipped the mule's feeding time, the animal protested loudly. The second day, it protested more feebly. The third day it was silent, and on the fourth, it dropped dead in harness right in front of the church. "Aiee, what bad luck!" the peasant wailed. "Just when I'd gotten it completely used to not eating!"

Paco stood up slowly. "Well, back to work or the orchard won't get plowed before the harvest starts," he said. "Once we start harvesting, there's no time for anything, and I don't know what kind of help we can hire this year either. There used to be sons enough in every family, and till four or five years ago, there were lots of good men waiting to be hired, but now all you get is people who can't do anything, who aren't worth paying."

"My husband and I might come help you," I offered.

"You'd get tired, you'd get dirty, it's not your work," they protested. Finally it was agreed we would come along one day to see for ourselves what it was like.

A few days later, barrels were being rolled out into the streets, scrubbed with hot salt water, and left to dry. Seven or eight barrels of 250 gallons each lie outside each house. The man of the house washes out the vat, the press, and the wooden buckets. There is an air of expectancy. The children, who have just returned from school, sense the mood. They make pests of themselves, hanging around the doorways, climbing on the barrels, and getting in the way of the work.

The harvest is almost over along the coast, across the foothills where the moderating effect of the Mediterranean ripens crops four or five weeks earlier. Migrants searching for work are moving toward us. September is a good time of year to lock the doors and be glad the ground-floor windows have iron grilles, our neighbors told us, because a great many people from elsewhere come by at harvest time. There is a word for them—*forasteros*, a term that encompasses not just strangers or foreigners but all people from another locality, whether it is New York, Japan, or the next village. *Forasteros* are received with courtesy and friendly smiles, just as we were, but they are watched until they prove themselves. All crimes (though there are almost none except for a rare case of petty theft) are committed by *forasteros;* at least, so every native will tell you.

Caravans of gypsies heading south go by in September. Gypsy women came to the village one day to buy bread and wine. Heads turned to watch them pass carrying baskets of the finest, whitest straw, swinging their long hair and full skirts, hoop earrings gleaming gold against black hair and dark orange skin. Their collection of babies, husbands, grandparents, and the single mule and cart hung with pots and pans and assorted bright-colored rags like the banners of a multinational gathering, were encamped down the road within sight. The villagers kept an eye on them until they moved on a day later.

The square in Riera used to be filled on September mornings with sun-blackened, lean, aquiline-faced men from the south, come with bundles on their heads to pick grapes for the relatively high wages of the north. In the last few days we had seen some walking the road with bundles of clothes on their backs, but there were fewer this year, the villagers said. Better wages and steadier jobs were easier to find now, thanks to the growing tourist boom. Some of the pickers who came by were not worth hiring. But while they might not find work, they were always given a coin or piece of bread in any house or shop.

No Spaniard ever turns a beggar away or questions his need. For years, every Sunday after mass, an old man who wore a peculiar homemade bandage cocked over one ear as he might have worn a favorite cap, knocked at every door of the village to announce loudly, "*¡Soy el pobre!* I am the beggar!" Everyone gave him something, and on market days one often stood in line with him in the marketplace in Riera where he was waiting to buy fish or meat or vegetables with the money he begged on Sunday. And why not? *¡Que viva!*—Let him live.

There are two drunks arguing in the street two houses down, this September evening. They have been there, arguing, since seven o'clock, and it is now ten-thirty. One is blind, the other is missing an arm. They appear every September, no one knows from where, looking for work picking grapes. Both are covered with a miscellany of jackets and old sacks, the whole fading into, blending with, inseparable from, a wad of clothes slung on their backs. Whether that is all they own or only traveling baggage, no one knows. Someone just asked them where they were going to sleep, but they were too busy arguing to answer. They are arguing about what day it is. One finally went up to a peasant passing in a cart to ask if it was not, in fact, Friday. Told it was, he went back to his companion, but the confirmation evidently bore little weight because the argument went on. Sometime during the night it stopped and the two men disappeared, to reappear the next morning with a dog. There was a new argument, this time about the dog. One claimed it would help them find work; the other said it would keep them from it. Whether the dog was to blame or not, no one hired them, but every peasant wife gave them money or food before sending them on.

"We had a time deciding whether to hire you or them," the Solés chuckled the next morning, "but you came out on top in the end."

The day was set for a week from Thursday. The harvest is always staggered in the village, covering a month or five weeks in all, because the peasants help each other, sharing hands, carts, and presses until everyone is finished, all the barrels are full, and all the vines stripped. During those four or five weeks, the entire village is devoted to the harvest, even those who have other professions. The carpenter dropped all his work. The shopkeepers left the grandmothers and children in charge of their shops (which made buying very confusing because neither the very old nor the very young could add at all well or remember prices, but at least no one did without the necessities, and accounts eventually got straightened out). Antonio, the barber, came back from the fields early on Friday and Saturday to cut the men's hair in the front room of his house, and the baker managed to bake bread every other night. Everyone had double work, especially the women, who were in the fields all day but had more work in the house than ever, more meals to prepare, more dirty clothes stiff with grape juice and stuck with tendrils and burrs, more dirt in the house from the coming and going of the men unloading and pressing grapes and from the carts going up and down, up and down, stirring the fine white dust of the street that filters through closed shutters. Dark red juice is splashed like bloodstains over the stone floors of the entrance to every house, and the smell of crushed grapes and fermenting wine is heady in the streets.

Every man made his own decision regarding the best time to harvest according to the risk he wanted to take.

Providing the weather held and the sun shone, the longer you waited, the higher the alcoholic content of the wine, and the better the pay for it. On the other hand, waiting beyond the day of ripening always meant increasing the risk of loss through rainstorms that brought rot, disease, and delay. Hail was the greatest disaster of all. Paco was gambling in waiting so long to start.

Not only for the Solés, but for everyone in the village, wine was the main income. Whether the year was good or bad hung on the harvest. For the month preceding it, everyone watched the skies. When the high mountain ridge that shadows the village in the late afternoon grows black with clouds, it will rain. Usually, however, winds crossing the plains from the Mediterranean or sweeping down from the high mountains to the north chase the gathering storm clouds away. Sometimes, too, the whole horizon is purple with rain while the village lies under a white, showerless bank.

"Too bad we haven't had a good shower," Paco remarked, "just enough to swell the grapes. You may find it hard to believe, but a light steady rain about now can almost double the harvest overnight. When that happens, we say it isn't raining rain, it's raining pesetas . . . At least the storm went by without dropping hail the way it did in Santa Colomna."

In that town, just over the mountains, all the grapes—all the work of the past year and all the livelihood of the next—were destroyed in a half-hour. A year of pruning, shaping, plowing, fertilizing, and walking up and down for days with the heavy tank of blue-tinted copper spray to stave off mildew—all that labor and money was wasted. The peasants shrugged. What can you do? That's the way it is.

"What will people in Santa Colomna do?" I asked Paco. "Will they have enough to eat?"

Paco smiled. "Every farmer has a year's harvest put away in case," he answered. "We know you have to expect the bad years along with the good."

The appointed Thursday came without either showers to swell the grapes or hail to destroy them. If the weather would just hold now till the harvest was in! Every day was as long as one could make it to get in as much as possible as quickly as possible, but always without hurry. No matter how urgent the task, I have never seen a peasant hurry in the fields.

When we set out in the cart, it was still dark, chilly, and damp, for it was already late September. The dew-covered vines quickly soaked our clothes, which stayed wet until the sun came out hot enough to dry them. It was harder and harder to work in the intense heat, though Sara remarked she thanked the Virgin Mary that women no longer had to wear skirts to the ground and heavy black hand-knit stockings as they had when she was a little girl. She recalled one scorching day when she and her sister had rolled their stockings down to their ankles. They had thought it wouldn't be noticed under the long skirts, but their father knew right away. It was a scandal, a disgrace to the family, and if they ever did it again, they'd get a beating to remember. The clothes had changed, but grape picking was the same. As we women moved in parallel order down the rows, returning to empty our heavy full baskets and start down the next row without a pause, the heftiest men shouldered the wooden buckets of grapes to the cart, where the mule stood stamping, whisking his tail, shaking his head, impatient with the heat and flies. The grape juice stuck to our arms, matted our hair, stained our clothing. The flies swarmed over the sweet stickiness, and the sun burned high in a metallic blue sky so still there was not a bird in motion. The tiredness increased. The back-aches from stooping—snip, snip, snip, cutting off the firm, heavy bunches of grapes, three or four in easy reach, then one or two more hidden behind thick clusters of leaves.

The carts go up and down all day, creaking and lurching, loaded with grapes, covered with flies, the horses sweating, the men wearing handkerchiefs tied under their straw hats to keep the sweat from running into their eyes, the women with kerchiefs over their hair, which gets stickier and gummier every day through the whole month of the harvest, but there's no point in washing it until the picking is over.

At the end of the long day, I was unable to imagine getting up before dawn the following morning to do the same again. I was surprised to find Sara felt the same way, though she got up and went because she had to. The first few days, she confessed, she always felt so tired that she thought it would be impossible to finish the day, impossible to start the next. But then, you somehow get used to the tiredness, she explained. It becomes part of you and you keep on, just as tired, but finding it easier somehow. Then, too, if it's a good harvest, spirits are high. People smile broadly and wave as they pass with carts creaking under their load of grapes. Wine was the backbone of the village, even though all the villagers complained that it didn't pay any more, and though the young people would take any road but the one to the vineyard.

Paco offered to press some grapes for us from the harvest so we could have our own barrel of wine in the house rather than having to buy it by the liter from the café. Delighted, we bought an old barrel and prepared it under his supervision, washing it out with salt, airing it in the street, and burning a stick of sulfur inside to purify it. Paco had his own press, as many villagers did, though a few were still trampling grapes with bare feet while they clung to a cord. Trampling grapes sounds like good messy fun, something on the order of finger painting, but people who have done it say the combination of breath-shortening effort and noxious fumes from the grapes makes it quite disagreeable. If a cat walks across the vat while the wine is fermenting, it will fall dead from the fumes, they say.

One afternoon, Paco stopped his grape-laden cart in front of our house and called out, "These are for you. From my best field, the one that still has *macabeo* grapes. They get more diseases, make more work, and you hardly get paid more for them, but they make the best wine."

He laughed at our expressions when we looked at the contents of the cart. What a wretched, sorry sight grapes are when they are brought in, piled up, stems and all, often still coated with chemical sprays, sometimes half rotted or partly dried into raisins, and all covered with flies, some of which drown in the sticky mass. "Don't worry, the alcohol takes care of everything," Paco said as he and the neighbors poured the grapes into the press.

Wine-making is a surprisingly simple process. Grapes are spread over round, woven rope mats, which are stacked in layers, one by one, in a cylindrical press about six feet high and three feet in diameter. The men push against what look like wagon wheel spokes jutting horizontally from the upper part of the cylinder, the press turns, and juice trickles down the sides into a groove in the floor leading to the underground vat. From there it is suctioned into barrels. Sometimes it is left in the vat to ferment, but Paco put ours directly into our barrel. The fermentation, he explained, would help cure the wood and improve the barrel. The filled barrel was carried to our house, where it was propped horizontally on wooden horses in the coolest part of the ground floor. If corked at this point, Paco told us, the barrel would explode when the wine began to ferment. Instead of a cork, he placed a chunk of olive-oil soap, made of residue from the olive pressing, over the hole in the top of the barrel but only half covering it.

"The sooner fermentation starts, the better the wine," Paco said. "It'll start within a week if the wine is going to be good."

We stopped by the barrel to listen several times a day. At the end of the second day, we were rewarded by the sound of the wine bubbling like water on a low boil. As the bubbling goes on, you gradually move the soap over until it covers the hole. When the bubbling stops, after a week or ten days, you can remove the soap and cork the barrel. The wine then remains untouched until November first, the traditional day for tasting. Then it is poured out, the residue in the barrel is removed, and the clarified wine is poured back to finish maturing. While it is not mature enough to be good by November first, men who know wine as the village peasants do can already predict its quality. By Christmas it is drinkable, though it will continue to improve steadily until spring or summer.

To know this much about wine is like knowing just enough of a foreign language to get by in traveling. So long as nothing unusual happens, all goes well. To know wine as the peasants do requires years of experience, while the science of wine making, or enology, is on quite another level and of no concern to peasants, who drink or sell their wine young, unbottled, and without chemical additives—natural wine, they call it. When you are used to natural wine, you notice the taste of chemicals in bottled wines.

Once you have seen how roughly it is handled in the making, you are apt to forget that wine is nevertheless a delicate thing. "Never lean on a barrel," Paco said, "and don't let anybody dust it either or put anything on top of it, because you'll risk turning the wine." He warned us to watch for chemical changes, for wine continues to live and change constantly. He also warned us to withdraw wine steadily and regularly. To withdraw a third of a barrel at one time might not only turn the wine, but render the barrel unfit for anything but vinegar thereafter. To leave the barrel half empty for a month or more without drawing wine from it was to run the same risk.

"Another thing about the harvest you should get to know," he added smiling, "is the celebration." And he invited us to his house to share the traditional feast celebrating the end of the harvest, a feast for all those who had shared the work.

We were thirteen at table, seven guests and the family: the grandparents, Paco, Sara, and their two children, Josefina and little Pepe, who had done nothing for the harvest except to get in the way after school. "*Malos, son todos malos*—all children are bad," his parents said resignedly, the way everyone did, and everyone was right. Village children ran wild until of an age to go to work, when they suddenly became sober, responsible little adults at fourteen. In a year Josefina would be fourteen, and from then until she married, she would work all day at the embroidery machine, sewing in the upstairs window, doing piecework to be delivered on market days to Riera. But for the moment, she was not expected to do so much as lend a hand in the kitchen.

The baker, Carlos Miret, and his wife, Rosetta, had been invited, along with their daughter Carmen, a placid, plump, freckled girl of sixteen with candid blue eyes and sun-flecked red hair. Sara's Aunt María was there with her husband, Raimondo, a jolly man in his mid-sixties to whom Paco often lent a helping hand. The hosts and guests, like most people in the village, were interrelated in a complicated way. It was impossible for an outsider to untangle all the relationships, but I learned that while the baker was not directly related to the Solés, Sara's aunt María, known to everyone as Tía María, was also the baker's aunt by marriage to Raimondo, his father's brother. Tía María was the mason's sister, I later discovered, and shared his stubborn strength.

Having had a heart attack, Raimondo, like José Solé, was no longer able to work in the fields. Far from bemoaning or apologizing for his disability, he thoroughly enjoyed it. Because of his fame in training partridges to call wild birds to a blind, he was constantly invited on expeditions by hunters and spent most of the season outdoors. He had had the good luck to sell at a fair price a strip of land near Riera where developers were building an apartment complex for factory workers. I don't know what the sum was, but to him it had meant independence.

"I live like a lord now," he said happily, his blue eyes twinkling. "All play, no work, no worries. I have my house, my garden, my carriage,"—he referred to the bright yellow cart and diminutive burro hitched outside the Solé house. When he was young, he and his yellow cart had been well known to all the people of the region, through which he traveled selling vegetables and fruit in the streets. "I always wore a white suit, a Panama hat, and a white gardenia in my buttonhole," he said one day, "and all the women from sixteen to sixty were in love with me. When I looked at a woman, my eyes were two burning lights, like the two headlights of a car or the beacon of a lighthouse.

"I have my sport, rich game to eat, and I'm well served." He glanced at Tía María, who smiled broadly, nodding her head with quick birdlike movements. "I have my club, too. Once a week I drive to Riera, have my hair cut, and sit with my cronies in our favorite café all morning, eating stewed tripe and drinking wine. What more could a man want?"

"Ah, it's good to be a man," Sara said placidly, cutting and passing huge chunks of *coca*, serving all the men first. *Coca*, a flat bread baked smothered with onions, sausages,

73

strips of red pepper, and as long as the harvest table itself, is the traditional opening dish at harvest dinners. You order it by the yard at the baker's, where you bring the trimmings for the baker to garnish the *coca* dough. I don't know how it became the harvest dish, but I can't think of a better way of combining the Mediterranean triad—the Biblical wine, bread, and olive oil—that has been the staple diet of the area for over 2,000 years. Unless you have eaten *coca*, hot and crunchy, with an unctuous purée of onions simmered in olive oil, and accented with peppery sausage, you cannot imagine how good it is, or how good it smells, or how well it goes with a nice dry white wine.

Paco was speculating about the price wine would bring that year. "When everybody has a good harvest, down goes the price, and we don't have a thing to say about it," he complained.

"I don't know what the government's thinking of," the baker remarked. "What would they do if there weren't any farmers? People aren't going to stay on the land if it doesn't pay." He looked at Paco's five-year-old son, who was squirming on his chair, giggly with wine. "Well, Pepe, are you going to be a farmer when you grow up?"

"No," the little boy said firmly, then tittered uncontrollably.

The adults smiled. It was normal for children to get high on wine at feasts, though on ordinary days they usually drank it cut with water. Wine is nourishing, villagers say. Everyone, young and old, drinks wine from toddling age or before, and usually at breakfast as well as other meals because coffee is still a luxury, while wine is cheap. In a restaurant a quart of wine costs less than twenty cents, and we paid less than half that for the wine in our barrel. Indeed, peasants were more apt to run out of water than wine. The baker told me that in the fields he had washed his hands in wine more than once, for lack of water.

"Good wine makes a good meal," the baker said contentedly, washing down another huge slice of *coca*. "But I never drank it as a child. I don't know what my father had against it. I've never found out to this day, but he never used to touch it. His friends teased and urged him, but they couldn't change his mind until one day some of them took hold of him—he's a big man, too, not easy to get hold of, but they managed. They tossed him into a full barrel of wine, head down, holding his head under till he had swallowed great gulps of it and was half drowned. Well, it was a funny thing. That changed him. He still won't drink wine at meals, but right after dinner he goes down to the cellar, makes the sign of the cross over the barrel with the words, 'in the name of the Son, the Father, and the Holy Ghost,' draws and drinks down a glass of wine, wipes his mouth with his sleeve, and says, 'Amen.'"

Old José Solé laughed, and he and Raimondo told story after story of the good old days, of drinking, singing, practical jokes, horseplay, and fights, too. Men carried knives and used them until the Civil War. The young from various villages fought each other in gangs; the men drank, became heated, quarreled, and fought among themselves. If a rare fight breaks out now, people call in the Guardia Civil, but in those days, as José Solé said, "The rich didn't care so long as it was only among us, so we settled things our own way."

"Unless somebody got killed," Raimondo put in. "Then the courts got into it. Do you remember Pedro?"

José Solé nodded.

"The rest of you are too young," Raimondo continued. "There was a man in Las Casas who was so jealous of this Pedro, he kept following him around, calling him a booby, weak-kneed, lily-livered, pigheaded, and I don't know what all. Pedro was a huge fellow, so big his fingers were twice the size of an ordinary man's. The judge said afterward

Pedro could have killed the man by just squeezing him with his left hand if he'd wanted to, but that wasn't the way it happened. Pedro kept his temper for weeks, months . . . I don't know how long. All he'd ever say was, 'Leave me alone, I won't have anything to do with you.' But one day this jealous man came up to Pedro in the street, pulled out a pistol, and fired it at close range without warning. Luckily for Pedro, the bullet just caught his trouser leg near the knee without hurting him a bit. He pulled his attacker off the ground with his left hand, while with his right, he stabbed up with a knife thrust so powerful the fellow flew up in the air like he was tossed from the horns of a bull!"

"I remember," José said. "Pedro got off at once because everyone knew the dead man brought it on himself."

"We had a good time," Raimondo said, "but we knew how to work, too."

"When I think how hard Father worked all his life . . ." Sara sighed. "Nobody does that now."

"It's too hard a life," Carmen put in with feeling.

"Yes," José said to Sara, "your father and Gorri and Carlat—I don't think Carlat ever slept. By two in the morning, he was too restless to stay in bed and had to be up doing something. The whole family's nervous like that. He always had to be the first—the first cart to pass, the first man to thresh, the first to start the harvest—a very nervous man."

"Is it his son's cart," I asked, "that passes long before the others, long before dawn every day?"

It was, they told me. "He must be able to see in the dark," said Paco, letting Sara heap his plate again with lamb chops she had broiled one by one in the fireplace on a tiny grill. There was the powerful *all-i-oli*, a garlic mayonnaise, to go with them, and potatoes fried in olive oil. "I never had to say no because of not being able to eat more," Paco remarked proudly. When he added that if guests at his house didn't eat a lot, he never invited them again, I took a second helping, too.

"It's a good life," said Carlos, the baker, "if you're strong, healthy—and have good land. If only I'd had good land, what I wouldn't have done with it!"

"We lived more like one family in the old days, too," Raimondo said, ignoring Carlos' plaint. "Paco, here, is always ready to help anybody out, though he's got as much work or more than anyone, but most people go their own way now and let the other fellow take care of himself. It doesn't work out as well."

"You can't get cooperation," Paco agreed. "Take the cart roads. There are some used by three, maybe four, maybe five families to get to their fields. The roads get so washed away in the rains you can hardly get over the stones. Why, with a full load from the harvest, you're apt to spill it if you don't fix the road up first. If we all got together to fix it, there'd be just two hours' work for everyone using it. But when you ask around, one man says he doesn't have time now, another claims he doesn't use it much, and so on, and why should you do all the work for the rest? So the roads stay as they are, though it'd be a lot easier for everyone to fix them." He sighed. "Ah well, it's as God wills."

Sara was passing stewed chicken while Paco opened the bottles of local champagne that inevitably accompany chicken at any local feast. Young Pepe, bored after two hours at table, was kicking the table legs so persistently he had to be threatened with the Guardia Civil, who had been around just that morning, Sara told him, asking for the names of bad little boys to be taken away.

"Nowadays people think they don't need neighbors, but they do," the baker said, nodding his head. "Just wait'll the chimney catches fire—then they'll see if they need neighbors or not."

77

"When I grow up," Josefina interrupted, "I'm not going to marry a peasant and live here. I'm going to live in a big city like Uncle Pablo and Aunt Rosa, or like Cousin Marina!"

"Uncle Pablo is Paco's cousin, who left for Barcelona years ago to become a taxi driver," Sara explained to me, "and often comes for weekends or holidays with his wife and daughter, Marina. Just because Marina's studying for her baccalaureate and lives in the city, Josefina wants to copy her in everything."

"Carmen's forever talking about her, too," said Rosetta.

"She's the only girl my age I ever see," Carmen protested.

"What does she want to do all that studying for?" Rosetta continued. "She'll just get married and forget it. She'll get thin studying so much."

Sara nodded, regarding her own substantial bulk with satisfaction. "Eat, Josefina," she said, pointing to a bit of chicken left on the young girl's plate, "or you'll never grow up to be a woman."

"She's much too thin, isn't she?" Grandmother Solé asked me. The girl looked quite normal to me for a thirteen-year-old. I answered ambiguously, "Just give her time."

"Could be," the grandmother remarked hopefully. "Take Sara here. She was a scrawny child and a thin young girl, too, but she turned out fine. *Gordo*," she added, using the word that means both handsome and fat, just as *beau* does in the south of France. Like all Catalan women over twenty-five, Sara probably weighed close to 170 pounds, which was apparently considered about right.

Homemade caramelized almonds were served along with raisins, walnuts, dried figs, and *vino rancio* (literally, rancid wine), a sweetish, aged wine the peasants keep for special occasions. The men, pouring cognac in their coffee, started telling jokes among themselves. Josefina, restless throughout the long meal, got permission to run out to join her play-mates. "I will too go to Barcelona when I grow up," she called back defiantly as she ran out the door. Her mother shook her head. "Young girls always get crazy ideas," she remarked, "but they get over them when they get mar-ried. Let her have her fun now, she'll be settled soon enough." She began to clear the dishes and carry them to the kitchen, where plates and glasses were already stacked high from the many courses and wines we had consumed. What can you do? That's the way it is.

4 ❧

Carmen

THE BAKERY was the village newspaper. The other main source of information was the village trumpeter, a government employee paid to communicate official news by walking the streets, usually at sunrise, sounding his trumpet at every third house, and intoning the announcement in a loud singsong. The announcement might be about village road repairs, to which each householder contributed labor or money, the annual vaccination of household dogs, the availability of a traveling government agricultural expert, a new tax, or one of the many administrative details affecting a farming village. The trumpeter was of service in an emergency too. Once he passed at 2:00 A.M. to order all men between sixteen and sixty out to fight a spreading forest fire in the nearby mountains. But for information about the outside world or about happenings in the village, the bakery was the unofficial center. It was there I would hear of all comings and goings in the village, or of a traffic accident on the Riera road, or of an uprising in Czechoslovakia. Because no one read newspapers, all events, great and small, near and far, were passed on by word of mouth.

The bakery was a natural center for this exchange of information because every village woman came there twice a day to buy bread. The wood benches along the walls were almost always lined with women waiting for bread or simply staying on to exchange gossip. It was a pleasant place to linger, particularly in winter when the huge baking room was warmed by the wall oven and filled with the comforting smell of pine boughs burning and bread baking. The worn wood troughs for mixing dough, the planks where the crusty loaves were stacked, the gleaming tiled floor and heavy ceiling beams made the room cozy and inviting. Rosetta, her round, maternal figure in a freshly starched blue and white smock, presided smilingly, dispensing bread and amiable comments, always at the same slow pace.

On weekdays Rosetta handled the bakery alone while Carmen worked at the embroidery machine upstairs. On Sundays, however, when a crowd of women arrived all at once between mass and Sunday dinner, Carmen came down to help. It was on one of those mornings that I began to know her better. That Sunday, Rosetta complimented me as usual on my as yet rather poor Spanish. "How lucky we can understand each other," she added as she slipped a newly baked loaf into the cotton bag I carried bread in, as all village women did. "It must be very sad not to be able to make yourself understood. Why, just yesterday, Carlos was plowing a field near the road when a man in a car stopped, got out with a camera, and tried to say something to him. Carlos stopped his mule and came over to the man, but couldn't make out what he wanted at all . . . not a single word." She shook her head sadly. "So he went back to his plow, but the man said something again, and again Carlos dropped what he was doing and came over to see what the man wanted. That went on, over and over, until finally, somehow, Carlos understood that what the man wanted was to take a picture of him plowing with his mule, but of course every time the man had tried to ask him if he could, Carlos had stopped plowing!"

Everyone laughed amid a sympathetic clicking of tongues. Another woman commented how many foreigners one saw around now, and told how a carful had stopped at a farmhouse down the road, all of them gesticulating and repeating "*fontana*" or something like that. The farmers, thinking the foreigners were asking the way to a town called Fontaner, kept telling them to go two kilometers straight ahead, then turn right and continue another six kilometers, while the foreigners, who spoke a word or two of Spanish mixed with Italian, kept saying that was too far, impossible, until finally it somehow came out they were looking for a water fountain, to fill up their car radiator and thermos bottles, and not for Fontaner at all.

"I'd be scared to go anywhere I didn't speak the language," Rosetta said. "But these foreigners don't seem to mind . . . You'd think they'd want to stay where they can make themselves understood. Anyway," she said, turning to me as the expert on all foreigners, "what do they come here for? Aren't things better in their own country? Aren't they better off than we are? We've seen it in the movies, they have everything. Then why would they want to come here?"

"For the sun, partly," I suggested.

"You mean they don't have any sun where they live?" the women chorused in astonishment.

When I told them of the gray, rainy weather in parts of northern Europe, they shook their heads. "How sad," they said, "how can one live without sun? If we have two cloudy days, we're unhappy." They felt very sorry for the poor foreigners, and pleased that Spain had something special to offer them.

Carmen remarked wistfully how nice it was to know foreign countries and foreign languages, adding that she would have liked to learn, but there was, of course, no chance to in the village, and anyway she would never go anywhere. "We're ignorant," the women agreed, "we know nothing." When I pointed out that everyone in the bakery spoke two languages, Catalan and Spanish, while few Americans spoke anything but English, they all discounted their bilingual upbringing because they took it for granted.

After the women left with their bread to get Sunday dinner ready, I stayed on, talking with Carmen about what she had studied in school—a little geography, religion, government, embroidery, sewing, and, of course, reading, writing, and arithmetic. She, in turn, asked a number of questions about life outside Spain. The questions surprised me. For the first time, I realized how narrow her horizons and knowledge were, and also how broad her tolerance and understanding, how quick and intuitive her mind.

During our talk, a particularly humble-looking peasant woman came in for bread. While Carmen interrupted our conversation to serve her, Rosetta turned to make a chalk mark on the debit side of the blackboard after the woman's name, but I noticed she only pretended to mark it.

"There's no point in adding a chalk mark," Rosetta said almost apologetically after the woman left. "It will just look worse to her and I know she'll never pay anyway because she can't. She's had hard luck. Her husband's sick, they have no money, and the poor people have no children to look after them. I can't begrudge them their bread." She sighed, adding what the villagers so often said, "*La salud es lo principal.* Health is the most important thing." To the villagers, health is the one capricious element that can transform otherwise rigidly stable lives.

"And are you still all alone?" Rosetta asked me, touching on what the villagers dreaded most after sickness. When I said my husband would be away on tour for another three weeks, she clicked her tongue. "Aren't you afraid, all alone

84

in that big house?" she asked. "Don't you want to have Carmen come sleep in the house to keep you company? She'd be glad to." I smiled. Paco's daughter, Josefina, had been offered me as companion, too. I was used to being alone, I answered, and besides, what was there to be afraid of? Nothing ever happened in the village. "Nothing," she agreed, "but there doesn't have to be anything to make you afraid. Fear makes itself."

All the women were still talking about my moving into the house alone, she told me. It had happened that just after we had concluded arrangements to rent the house, my husband had had to leave for Paris. I had therefore picked up the baggage we had left in Barcelona and settled in with it alone. "We couldn't get over your arriving by yourself," Rosetta said, "in a village you didn't know, at night, too, and sleeping alone in a strange house, unafraid." "It's all just a matter of custom," I replied in village terms.

Rosetta and Carmen nodded. They were learning of other customs from seeing foreign women passing through Riera, they said. The first time they had seen one driving a car, they had exclaimed, "A woman driving a car! That's impossible!" Now they would remark instead that a woman could drive a car perfectly well, though Rosetta added she would never dare try it. Carmen, to the contrary, expressed a desire to learn and I arranged to show her and also to start teaching her French.

From that Sunday on, Carmen was often in our house. The more I saw of her, the more I was struck by her intelligence, tact, and taste. She learned French quickly, well enough to speak it with our occasional French visitors. While most village girls, and most of the women, would have fled in shyness at the appearance of outsiders, Carmen was interested in meeting them, poised in their presence, and shrewd in her comments afterward. She seemed to have little in common with the other young girls of the village, giggling young girls who would grow into smiling, hard-working, good-humored, but dull women.

One day after I had known Carmen for two years, I had a letter from a French couple with two small children who had visited Las Casas. They asked if Carmen might come to Paris for a year to help care for the children while living as part of the family and perfecting her French. I was delighted at the thought that Carmen might be able to leave the village, which I felt had too limited a horizon for her curiosity and intelligence. However, it was almost certain her parents would not agree. By tradition, girls left home only to marry. Not wanting to raise Carmen's hopes only to disappoint her, I mentioned the offer to her parents first.

Carlos and Rosetta presented themselves at the house with solemn faces. That they had been invited to come alone meant that something grave was going to be discussed, but there was no question of broaching the subject at once. For at least forty minutes, we exchanged chitchat while sipping wine and eating toasted almonds and home-cured olives flavored with wild thyme. When a significant pause fell, I knew it was time to let them know why I had asked them to come.

To my surprise, Carlos spoke without hesitation, "It's a wonderful chance for Carmen. I won't stop her if she wants to go." Rosetta had to yield, though tearfully declaring Paris was too far away. "But ask Carmen, it's her decision," Carlos added, smiling enigmatically. "We'll see what she says."

My second surprise was Carmen's equally unhesitating refusal. She couldn't leave her parents for a whole year, she would be too homesick so far away. It was an opportunity, she recognized that, but she would be unhappy accepting it. "Once I said yes, I'd have to stay on no matter how I felt," she said. Had it been for only a few weeks or perhaps even a summer . . . but a year, a whole year . . .

she couldn't even bear thinking about it and was only happy again when the subject was dropped.

It was probably just as well, I reflected afterward. Why should she be exposed to new horizons only to learn to be discontented? Going abroad for a year might make her dissatisfied with her present life, to which she would return, no longer a simple village girl, yet having no opportunity to become anything else either. It was best to leave things alone.

Limited though it was, Carmen seemed content with her life in the village, working at the embroidery machine beside her mother, helping her mother in the house, giggling with the other girls in the streets at night while going to fetch goat's milk, accompanying her mother to mass on Sunday mornings, and taking a walk down the Riera road on Sunday afternoons. The only lack she felt was the absence of companions her own age. There were no suitable beaux, and all the girls were either younger or much older than she because she happened to be one of the first born in the village after the upheavals of the Civil War and the long absence of the village men. Paco's cousin's daughter, Marina, was the only friend her age Carmen had. It was therefore natural that they should become close even though Marina's visits from Barcelona were short and infrequent, and even though Carmen resented Marina's superior airs.

When Marina invited Carmen to visit her in Barcelona for a week, there was great excitement in the baker's house. In her relief that there was no more talk of Paris, Rosetta was glad to agree. The preparations took weeks. Shoes were mended, a purse of Rosetta's refurbished, a new dress made by the village seamstress, a small cardboard suitcase bought, and arrangements completed by mail for Marina and her parents to meet the bus from Riera. Rosetta, who had not been to Barcelona for thirty years, not since a two-day honeymoon in the undreamed-of and hazily remembered luxury of a hotel room with a carpet and running water, was to accompany Carmen on the bus and spend the day in the city. It was hard to say which of the two was the more eager, though Rosetta's enthusiasm was occasionally over-shadowed by fears of not being met, of getting lost, of an accident on the road, or some other calamity.

"Ay, Barcelona!" Rosetta wrung her hands. "You couldn't get me to stay there for anything! It makes you dizzy, all those people everywhere. Why so many people? And cars. You'll be run over if you don't watch all the time crossing streets. And the noise! Here, at least, it's quiet, maybe too quiet, but in Barcelona—there's no living with noise like that. And so many people, so many buildings . . . It all closes in on you. I felt I couldn't breathe . . . I couldn't leave it soon enough!

"What did we do? We walked. We walked and walked, looking at shops and streets and buildings. Oh, yes, there's plenty to see, but I had such blisters because I never wear high heels here except maybe for a few hours some special day. And my dress was so tight I didn't dare eat lunch hardly when we finally stopped walking for a bit . . ." Rosetta's large bulk usually floated comfortably in a smock-like dress called a *bata*, but when she set off for Barcelona wearing her fitted black taffeta dress, she had looked like a sausage in a tight casing. "You know," she smiled, "be-cause we always wear smocks here, we never realize how fat we've gotten until a fiesta or a funeral comes along and we have to put on our best dress again. But in Barcelona, people dress up all the time. I don't know how people can live there. Also, I wouldn't spend a single night in Marina's family's apartment, it's so dark and small. Even where there are windows, they look out on nothing but a wall, because the buildings are all right next to one another. Ay, Barce-lona!"

88

Soon after Carmen came back, we set off together for an afternoon of mushroom hunting in the rocky hills behind the village. It was the kind of day on which it is hard to stop smiling. Wild thyme and rosemary were in pungent flower, the hot sun sent shafts of warmth through the cool October air, and the village sprawled below us in a valley of peace. The hills are so steep we had a bird's-eye view after a few minutes' climb, along with the feeling we were heading straight up into the deep blue of the sky, but the terrain became slow and difficult as soon as we left the goatherd's path to look for mushrooms among the scrubby pines and *pinchos*. *Pinchos* are sharply spiked evergreens that rake the skin mercilessly, but they are useful for cleaning chimneys, Carmen told me. An uprooted *pincho* tied at the top and bottom of a long rope is passed up and down the chimney by two men, one standing on the roof, the other in the fireplace.

There are many useful plants in the mountains—flowers to keep away flies and mosquitoes, herbs to cure or prevent every ailment—but Carmen, I discovered, knew little about them. People find it easier to go to the pharmacy or the hardware store, she told me. Only a few of the old men, like Raimondo and José, still know and gather herbs, tying fragrant bundles to the attic rafters for rheumatism, rashes, sprains, and flu. It struck me that the narrow world of the village was even narrower for young people like Carmen, who no longer knew the names and uses of the plants around them or the signs of the weather, or any of the folklore surrounding fiestas and work that had been passed on from one generation to another for centuries.

As we filled our baskets with mushrooms, Carmen told me her impressions of Barcelona. "I had no idea there were so many things, so many possibilities, so many choices," she said. "Now my eyes are opened." Through Marina she had met girls her age, nineteen and twenty, who were working in Barcelona, living in their own apartments, making their own way, putting themselves through school, and having fun doing it all. They went to concerts, theaters, movies; they knew groups of young people; they planned and worked toward humble careers as private secretaries, nurses, grade-school teachers. "I used to say I wished I had had a chance to learn this or that," Carmen said. "In Barcelona I met girls as old as I am or older who are just starting on their baccalaureates. Even though it'll take them years to get a degree others might have at seventeen or eighteen, they'll do it. It's a hard life, working and studying, but they have fun, too. There's no end of things to do in Barcelona. Even if I didn't have money to go anyplace, I could just walk and look for a month of Sundays."

In her brief visit, Carmen had asked dozens of questions. She knew how the other girls managed, how they had found jobs, apartments, had got into schools. It was clear it was not idle curiosity that had led her to ask so many questions. While Barcelona had seemed oppressive and closed to Rosetta, to Carmen it beckoned like an open door. It was only a matter of time, I thought, before she went through it.

How short that time would be, I had not guessed. At Christmas Carmen confided to me that she had met a girl from Riera who needed an additional roommate to pay the rent in Barcelona. For the January festival of the Three Kings, the traditional holiday for giving gifts in Spain, Carmen had got a two-week job as extra clerk in a toy store owned by friends of Marina's parents. While working there and living at Marina's apartment, she found a permanent job as receptionist and applied for midterm entrance in school. It all happened so fast that Rosetta was too stunned to make a vigorous stand.

"It's too far," she objected.

"Not as far as Paris," Carlos said.

"She's too young," Rosetta said.

"She's going on twenty," Carlos replied. "She's really too old to start working for a baccalaureate degree, but better late than never. Besides, she has a good head, she's sensible, and Marina's family will look after her."

"Ah, Marina," Rosetta said resentfully. "If it weren't for her . . ."

"Perhaps. But then, what future does Carmen have here? I'd have given anything to have a chance like this. We have to sacrifice our feelings."

Carlos' voice prevailed and Carmen left, all her belongings fitting in the same little cardboard suitcase with which she had made her first visit to Barcelona four months earlier. All the neighbor women cried in pity for Rosetta as they waved Carmen good-bye. "She won't like it, she'll be right back," they said in consolation.

5 &

Homecoming

EVERYONE WHO has relatives in the village or has once lived there comes back, if possible, for the village fiesta. Despite the predictions of the neighbor women, Carmen did not come running home to Las Casas, but she was there for the fiesta, the first year and every year after. Marina and her parents always came too, the first to arrive, in an enormous square old taxi painted green that hurtled honking down the street before dawn. The shouts of the two families greeting each other and slamming doors woke up anyone still asleep, and from then on, the early morning hours were filled with more joyous honking of cars and taxis pulling up filled with aunts, uncles, brothers, sisters, and cousins, as relatives arrived by train, bus, and car from all parts. From time to time, you could hear the frantic squawks of a hen being corralled for the sacrificial feast. The women, already exhausted from whitewashing, housecleaning, and making new clothes for themselves and their children, would spend most of the next few days in the kitchen. Cheerfully. *Es así,* that's the way it is, they say.

Every village, town, and city in Spain has an annual

fiesta mayor in honor of its patron saint, a holiday that lasts two, three, or even four days if the town is large enough. Las Casas was too small to fill three days with activities, but it tried to, out of pride. Out of practicality, however, it transferred the holiday from the name saint's day to a weekend so that relatives from near and far, and pleasure seekers from neighboring towns, would be free to swell the thin crowd.

The patron saints of most villages were fortuitously born in August, which villagers call the vacation month. There is always work to be done but, except for the feeding of the animals, it is the kind of work that can be put off for a day or a week unless rain necessitates spraying against the multiple plagues that thrive in humid heat. There are sweet melons to be gathered, carted to market, and sold; tools to be mended, and repairs made to the house; onions to be stored and tomatoes strung for winter, and the harvest of the earliest almonds to be shaken out of the trees by beating them with long canes.

The fiesta creates its own work. Every house is scrubbed and whitewashed. Even the entrance through which the mule passes, where the cart stands tilted like an upturned wheelbarrow and the greens for the animals are stacked, where piles of almond shells are heaped around a table at which the family sits shelling almonds before supper—even this room is whitewashed or bluewashed or yellowwashed. Blue is believed to discourage flies and mosquitoes, yellow hides the smoke stains from the kitchen fireplace, but white is the most beautiful. When the outside walls are whitewashed, they are so brilliant in the sun that they blind you with sharp stabs of light. Inside, the walls have more whites than Utrillo's palette, turning brown, blue, green, yellow, or rose in the light and passing through every shade of darkness. Carmen, who arrived several days before the fiesta to help her mother whitewash, clean, and prepare, already saw the beauty of these walls through outsider's eyes, and felt the rustic charm of her house with the spacious baking room downstairs and cozy, low-ceilinged rooms above.

The fiesta always started in our house, we learned our first summer in Las Casas. The holiday occurred just a few weeks after we had moved in. The night before I went to the bakery to buy the sweet, flat, anise-flavored breads made each year especially for the occasion. While I was there, Carmen mentioned that the young girls of the village traditionally assembled at our house to await the band that led the procession to the church for the annual blessing of the bread. Now that we had come, she confided, they did not know where to go. "To our house, of course," I said at once, asking what I was supposed to do for the occasion. "Nothing," she replied. Amalia, the Spaniard from Estremadura who worked for us, keeping the house clean and frying quantities of fish and potatoes for every meal, had other views. She scrubbed the entrance till it gleamed, swabbed it with olive oil to make it shine more, brought the best and largest pots of flowers in from the garden patio, lined the walls with all the chairs in the house, and swept and sprinkled the street in front of the house until the loose dust was turned into a firm, clean surface. I set out a five-pound box of cookies, which became a permanent, if not traditional, part of the fiesta every year thereafter.

The first timid little girls turn up at the door about nine in the morning, each carrying one of those long, flat anise breads decorated with flowers on a lace-covered wooden plank. Shyly they set down their breads and accept a cookie apiece. All wear new dresses made for the fiesta and white lace mantillas mounted on high combs with red carnations at one side. The schoolteacher's daughter wears white gloves, as befits her superiority.

Little by little, more girls arrive, then a few young boys, looking stiff in ties and jackets, a few dogs, and, lastly, the

95

señoritas of the village, marriageable virgins aged fourteen and up. The first year Carmen came back from Barcelona, she was the oldest, at twenty, and hardly marriageable anymore in village eyes; any village girl over nineteen who has not found a fiancé is usually doomed to spinsterhood.

As the entrance fills, the shy silence of the first arrivals is replaced by squeals, giggles, and excited talk that echoes off the thick stone walls. Cookies begin disappearing a fistful at a time.

A group of mothers, fathers, and older boys assemble in the street, which is enlivened by huge banners fluttering from the second-story windows of every house. The banners are the families' prize bedspreads—hand-embroidered roses on white satin, delicate lace stretched over scarlet silk, Victorian cotton crocheted over deep blue—all handmade by a member of the family, some over a hundred years ago.

Then the band arrives, emphatic and discordant, preceded by the priest and choirboys carrying a gaudily dressed statue of the Virgin. Mothers hastily pull their children away from the cookie supply and into a double line. With the band in front, the girls with their breads next, and the rest of the village falling in behind, the procession sets off for the church.

The mass at which the breads are blessed ends the religious portion of the holiday. Immediately afterward, the village repairs to the café for aperitifs. A concert is given by the best available orchestra, hired for the main feature of this and every village fiesta, the dance, or rather dances. In Las Casas del Torrente, in addition to the noon concert, there is a 7:00 P.M. "afternoon" dance, which lasts till 10:00, and a second concert about midnight, followed by the "evening" dance, which goes on until three or four in the morning. Everyone stays late out of a sense of duty, because how late everyone stays is the measure of the evening's success. Most villagers feel obliged to make the fiesta a success even if it no longer arouses much enthusiasm among a people recently exposed to radio and television and the novel distractions of towns and cities. A few villagers give the fiesta so little importance that they go to the fields as if these days were like all others. "That would never have happened in my time," Señor José said scornfully. "Why work today? Isn't there a tomorrow?"

The same program is repeated each of the three days of the fiesta in Las Casas, but to make it seem more varied, every dance is given a title to eclipse the previous one on the announcements posted at the café and distributed in neighboring villages. The *Gran Baile*, or Big Ball, is followed by the *Magnifico Baile*, which is succeeded by the *Gran Baile Extraordinario*. The same people attend and the same orchestra plays at each in the same place with the same decor and, for the most part, the same music.

Huge meals take up the interludes between dances. After we had lived in the village for a year, we were asked to various houses, and though we managed to accept no more than one invitation a day, we were always hard put to eat enough to give our hosts full satisfaction.

The year Carmen moved to Barcelona, we were invited to dinner at the baker's house the first day of the fiesta to celebrate her visit home. It was during that dinner that I came to understand how serious a break with tradition Carmen's departure from the village represented.

Although she wrote her parents often and in detail, Carmen's visits home had become less and less frequent as she became absorbed in her new life. One day, after she had been away four months, I saw a gleaming new washing machine standing proudly in a corner of the bakery. At the sacrifice, I am sure, of many meals, Carmen had saved enough to buy the machine for her mother so that she would no longer have the problem of carting the heavy laundry alone the long distance to the village vats.

Rosetta kept me informed of all Carmen's news. One day she told me Carmen planned to move to a new apartment in order to avoid spending three dollars a month on the subway, and to save a half-hour's travel each way. The saving of money Rosetta could understand, but the economy of a half-hour amused her. "Here we don't think anything of half an hour more or less, it's of no importance. But I can see life's very different there in Barcelona. Every minute of the day is taken up running from work to one class and another, and then home to study. She says there's hardly time to eat and sleep, and in the new apartment she'll be able to get up half an hour later." Rosetta smiled indulgently. "At home she used to sit for hours at the table after dinner and could never get up before ten, she was always so sleepy. I can't picture her being up at 6:30 every day. How suddenly she changed, and how completely!"

At dinner on the day of Carmen's first homecoming for the *fiesta mayor,* she confessed how much she dreaded going to the dances. There were no young people her age, she complained. Her mother insisted that missing any part of the fiesta was unthinkable. 'It matters to us, we live here," she said.

Carmen sighed in acquiescence. "Here everyone knows everything about everyone else," she said. "From the time you're born, the village knows everything you do. It's so much easier to be yourself in Barcelona, where nobody knows you and nobody cares."

"It can be lonely if nobody cares," her mother said.

Carmen shrugged. "I'm not lonely."

"You're young," the baker said. "There's a lot you don't know yet. It's hard to understand anything you haven't lived. For instance," he turned to me, "it's hard for people here to understand why we'd let Carmen go to Barcelona or why she'd want to."

Most of the old people in the village had never been to

Barcelona, though it was only thirty miles away. Before television, they had no idea what it looked like either—a larger, noisier Riera, they supposed, and they shook their heads in pity for the people who had to live there. In Rosetta's mother's day, village girls were often sent to Barcelona to be servants until they married, but they were always placed with a family known to some relative, and the family saw that the doors were locked after dark and that the girls were working or chaperoned at all times. No girl, then or now, ever left to make a career or live on her own or leave her parents, and for the last forty years, none has left Las Casas to go into domestic service either, because there has been work in the village aside from field work.

First came the knitting factory, not really a factory at all, just a big peasant house rented by an outsider who paid women a pittance to knit and package long woolen underwear, scarves, and caps for winter, and the heavy black wool stockings all women wore all year from age twelve on. About forty of them worked there at one time, Rosetta said. But after a while, hand-knitting no longer paid, the factory closed, and other outsiders began doling out piecework to be done on knitting machines.

I had seen Sara's knitting machine, upstairs in the Solé house. It had hardly paid for itself, she said. The women had to buy their own machines, learn how to run them, pay for their own materials, and turn out each week, in whatever quantities the buyers demanded (always either too little or too much), exact replicas of sample baby caps, scarves, knit suits, bootees, and other apparel, all of which were shipped off, never to be seen in local stores. There was little money to be made on the machine unless you became very rapid, changing the threads so quickly that the gestures were almost invisible, and, even then, you had to spend most of the day at it—eight, ten hours or more, as all the young girls did after leaving the one-room school-house at age fourteen. One day, work on the knitting machines became scarce, to no one's very great surprise, since all the women would tell you the machine-knit work looked very nice but, once washed, was likely to fall apart. That's the way it was ordered and that's the way they made it, without giving it a thought except to wonder where it was sent. "Such flimsy things," they said to each other. "Where does it go? Who buys it?"

"Carmen was fast on the knitting machine and one of the first to change to machine embroidery," Rosetta said. "She got really good at it, turning out piles of work. We used to work side by side, but she always did twice as much."

One week it was five hundred pillowcases with blue and pink angels hovering, index finger to lips, around a sleeping child; another week, there was an equal number of table doilies with livid orange and blue daisies on stiff stalks. It helped to pass the time, the women said, for young girls until marriage, for married women with odd moments free, and it filled the long winter days when there was little work to be done outside the house. No woman expected anything better than this monotonous, poorly paid piece-work or whatever would come to replace it. *Que haremos? Es así.* What can you do? That's the way it is. Most were glad they were born in an era when they did not have to do the hard work of the fields except for harvests and a few particularly busy times.

"Weren't we happy here together?" Rosetta asked Carmen. "Wasn't it enough for you?"

"Sometimes I think back to when I was sixteen, sitting here all day embroidering and knowing what would happen tomorrow and the next day," Carmen answered almost dreamily. "Sometimes I think I didn't know how well off I was, how happy and untroubled. But I could never go back to being happy and peaceful in the village now. I've changed too much."

"It's a beautiful village," I said.

"Sometimes I think so," she answered. "And sometimes, when I first see it again, coming in on the bus, I wonder if there's anything sadder on earth. At noon the houses are all stretched out, mud-colored and flat, without a tree for shade, burning up in the sun. And at night it's sadder still. All you can see are a few dim lights, so low they're more red than yellow. In summer, at least, there are people in the streets, sitting in doorways, talking, and that livens it a bit, but in winter there isn't a living soul after sundown. Everyone's in his house and everyone goes to bed right after supper.

"Then, too, in Barcelona I have so much to do, I never have time to think, but here, after a day or two, though I love seeing mother and father, I don't know what to do anymore."

Over Carmen's protests, Rosetta heaped her plate again with roast duck, gravy, and potatoes fried in olive oil. Carmen, who had changed in half a year from a plump girl to a lovely, slim young woman, sighed in despair.

"You're getting too thin in Barcelona. You work too hard and probably don't eat enough, living on your own, running around keeping a job and putting yourself through school, the Virgin Mary knows what for," Rosetta said.

"An education is everything," her husband interrupted. "If I had had a chance . . ."

"You need someone to look after you," Rosetta continued, handing her daughter a thick slice of bread to mop up the gravy on her plate. "I've often thought we ought to all move to Barcelona now you're there."

"You wouldn't like it," Carmen said hastily. "You'd be lost there."

"Maybe," her mother sighed. "Made me dizzy just to

visit for a day, it's so noisy, dirty, and big, with people in such a hurry they don't have time to stop and talk. Even Riera's too crowded for me now. Why, you have to look both ways before you cross a street now, there're so many cars . . . But what's to become of us in our old age alone?"

"Ah, we'll see. We're not old yet," her husband put in. "I'd have liked a chance to do what Carmen's doing when I was young. Once a friend and I were going to stow away on a ship to South America—I was living with an uncle in Barcelona, helping in his store—but I went back to my room to get something, and when I got to the wharf, the ship had gone with my friend on it. Never heard from him again. Maybe he made a fortune in South America. Maybe I'd have made a fortune if I'd gone."

"What more do we want?" Rosetta said. Talk of faraway places made her nervous. "We have our own house, our own vegetables, wine, food, a fire in winter, independence— what more do we want?"

"It's all right for us," the baker agreed. "We don't need much. But for Carmen there's no life in the village."

"She's not the only one. Little Josefina Solé has ideas about going off to Barcelona, too, though her parents will never let her."

"If I'd gotten married, I'd have left home, too," Carmen said.

"Naturally, but that would be different," her mother answered. "You'll never want to come back?"

"To visit, yes. Always. But not to stay. I couldn't live here now."

"But just what are you going to do once you get your education?" Rosetta asked.

"I can't say now," Carmen answered, "because I can only see a little way ahead. Once I get my baccalaureate, I can get a better job, earn enough to live and study by working only part-time, and then I can advance a little faster and raise my ambitions a bit higher. For now, all I can hope to do is keep my job as a receptionist, because it allows me to do a bit of studying during the eight hours." She sighed. "When I think back, I see how much time I wasted, but I was content, so content I might never have found out what I was missing or that I was missing anything, if it hadn't been for Marina and her friends."

"Ah, Marina," Rosetta sighed without bitterness. "She started it all."

"I guess so," Carmen said. "Before, I didn't want anything more. Now I want something else all the time. Still, I'd never change back."

"What will become of us?" Rosetta said again, almost to herself, shaking her head as she went to the kitchen to fetch an enormous casserole of veal and home-dried wild mushrooms.

What would become of Carmen if she came back? Coming back would mean returning to the life she had when she was fourteen, fifteen, sixteen, and a lifetime of the same if she never married: embroidering on the sewing machine next to the light from the window, upstairs, beside her mother, all day until sunset, when she would go fetch the goats' milk, greet the old men and women sitting in their doorways, and make plans for Sunday, the only day that varied in the week. For her, though, there were no village boys to date on Sunday. Unless she found a fiancé in a neighboring town, and that was less likely every year, what she had done every day since leaving school was what she would do when she was forty-two or sixty-two . . .

At the dance that afternoon, Carmen sat on the sidelines with the older couples and black-garbed widows in the boxes for spectators, who were as many and as long-staying as the dancers, though it was impossible to talk in the boxes because the band, playing at full blast, had added a public-address system to triple the decibels, to everyone's apparent satisfaction. "It's too quiet here most of the time anyway," one villager commented. On the dance floor, the few married couples over thirty who still danced waltzed stiffly among a flock of teen-agers who were clumsily aping the latest hit dances and a bevy of three- and four-year-old toddlers who imitated the dancers or darted between their legs. To sit through all six dances of the three-day fiesta as a spectator was an ordeal I did not envy Carmen.

The women in our box and the next boxes greeted Carmen warmly. "So you haven't forgotten Las Casas . . . So you remembered us . . . But how thin you've gotten! Aren't you afraid living by yourself?"

"Afraid of what?" Carmen asked.

"Of anything, of everything. Don't you miss home and your parents?" Beneath their friendliness lay unspoken disapproval.

The wall around the village was an invisible one, yet anyone could see the breach Carmen had opened, a breach through which others might follow.

6

Old Age

ALMOST ANY pleasant afternoon, on top of the hill over-shadowing the village, you could come across the oldest man in town, the baker's father, Alfonso Miret. You would find him sitting on a rock under a pine tree, singing to himself, tapping his cane in the dust, pausing to greet everyone who passed going to and from the fields or to the next village.

"*Appa*, have a good day. Hot? A little, maybe, but not very." He wore, as always, a black wool beret, a black wool and rayon vest over a striped shirt, and the customary long, wide black cummerbund wrapped round and round his waist. In the old days, he carried a knife in it. There were no more knives; no knives and no singing anymore.

"How we used to sing in the café every Saturday and Sunday," he told me as I sat down beside him to chat and enjoy the light breeze through the pine boughs. "Sing, laugh, drink, fight . . . There's no life in people anymore. In the café, there's the television so loud you can hardly play cards or hear yourself talk, and a few people sitting by themselves looking at it, and a lot of silence around.

Fewer and fewer people, too. When I was young, we were poor, so poor that from time to time, one of us wouldn't have enough for a glass of wine, but we'd go anyway, pocket and glass empty, to sit at the table for the company, singing, and jokes, every Saturday, Sunday, and holiday. If you didn't have the money, you didn't have the wine either, because no one had an extra peseta to buy you any. Sundays were the liveliest because people used to come from miles around to dance to the player piano. There are still some of us around who remember, but we don't fill a table now. I've heard rumors the village council is thinking of closing the café because it's not worth paying anyone to run it for a few people. And then where would we go? Well," he smiled, "by that time I'll probably have gone down the road to the cemetery. Maybe my friends will be there, too, so there won't be any problem. Let the young take care of the problems anyway, just as they take care of me."

Sara Solé came down the road, wiping her round, smiling face with a large checkered handkerchief, balancing a bundle of greens tied up in a large cloth on her head.

"It's hot," she said, stopping in the shade beside the old man.

"*Appa*, a little maybe, not so very," Alfonso answered.

"Here it's better," she said, sitting down on a stone. "That's a good comfortable stone," she remarked a moment later, after thinking it over. "When the carpenter came to repair my chair today, he wanted 75 pesetas for it [about $1.10]. Imagine! An old chair like that. It's not worth it. Besides, there isn't any point in paying to fix a chair when a stone will do just as well, so I sent him along."

Alfonso Miret had started to sing softly again and wasn't listening.

"I wanted to get greens for the goat before taking the afternoon bus to Riera," Sara said. "Josefina needs a new suit. Seems she's always needing something new. It's the age, of course—sixteen . . . though when I was that age we never spent any money unless we had to."

"Ah, young people," Alfonso commented.

"But the worst of it is, they're leaving," she continued. "Look at Raimondo and Tía María. With their only son living in Riera, who's to take care of them now she's fallen sick? Raimondo can't do any work, and now neither can she. I think she has something bad."

Whenever I thought of Tía María, I saw her erect, wiry, striding the six miles to Riera in rain or blazing sun in her black cotton dress. Just three weeks before, I had come across her on the road to Riera with a heavy basket on her head. Hoping for a return ride, she asked as she got in the car if I had much to do in town. It was so hot that her rope-soled shoes had been sinking into the melting asphalt of the highway. "Very little," I answered. "All I have to do is buy some rabbits for supper in the market. And you?" She started to laugh in her clear, chirping voice. "Buy rabbits?" she said. "I was going to Riera to sell rabbits!" She tapped the basket. "How many did you want?" When we discovered I had set out to buy three rabbits and she to sell three rabbits, I pulled over to the side of the road, partly because I was laughing so hard and partly because there was no point in going any farther. We concluded the sale there at the side of the road, turned around, and headed back, mission accomplished.

"I can't imagine Tía María sick, somehow," I said.

The old man shrugged. "We all have to die," he said. He was not concerned. His son and daughter-in-law would take care of him. He'd seen to that, I'd heard. It was even written out in an official paper he'd made, leaving the bakery and land to them on the condition he lack nothing in his old age. He was no fool. He had his meals, clean clothes, medicine, money for the café and for the cigars they kept begging him to stop smoking—everything he needed, he'd arranged for, and the rest was as God willed.

"You're lucky," Sara said, "but some people aren't. You take care of your young when they're little and helpless; then when you're old and helpless, they turn their backs on you. There's no responsibility today."

"Ah, young people," Alfonso said again, content with himself and the world. "Till tomorrow," he added as Sara and I got up to walk to the village together, "if God wills."

"Now there's a happy old man," Sara said. "It's a good time of life if you're healthy and cared for. So many men never reach it. They work and then one day they die without ever being sick in their lives or taking a day off . . . They have their vacation in the grave."

Sara's parents had taken care of her grandparents in their old age, just as her sister now took care of them, while she and Paco took care of Paco's mother and father. That was the village way, or had been, and it seemed a good one to Sara. "Except," she remarked, making a face, "it's easier to live with your own mother like my sister does. She can come and go about as she pleases. Not that I'm complaining, but it just isn't quite the same as with your own mother."

I nodded, remembering the trouble we always had getting Sara to come on an expedition to town or a picnic. When she stopped at the bakery for bread, I walked on to the house thinking about it. In the old days of large families, every house was filled with sons and daughters and with their husbands and wives. Because there is often only one son in the house now, his wife, like Sara, has to face her mother-in-law alone, and the strain is visible. Grandmother Solé helps with the house and children, but she also rules the household, governs expenditures, and objects to too much frivolity on the part of her daughter-in-law. Having

grown up in an age when women stayed home, the grandmother is likely to view going anywhere other than to the
store, the fields, church, and village fiestas as frivolous.

The women here make no effort to look or act young as
they grow older. At thirty they are often in black for one
relative or another, and by the time they are fifty, they
are in mourning so much they no longer bother to buy
anything colored. Amalia was unable to contain her amusement at one of our Parisian guests, a woman of about fifty-
five, smartly dressed in pale yellow, with a carefully studied
coiffure. "She dresses her hair and paints her face," Amalia
commented to me in private, snickering. "Yes, well . . . ?"
I replied, puzzled. "Whatever for?" Amalia retorted, over-
come by giggles.

When old, ill, and widowed, the grandmother sometimes becomes a tyrant, a black shadow dominating the
lives of a couple in the prime of life. Possessed by the fear
of being alone that all village women seem to share, and
refusing to leave the house because of age, illness, or
simply the feeling that it is unsuitable for a widow, she
will try to keep everyone else from leaving. By words,
tearful reproaches, or attacks of illness, she claims constant
company as her due.

The baker's sister, caring for her husband's bedridden
mother, could barely leave the house long enough to buy
at the village store. She would sigh and say, *"Es así, que
haremos?* We have to accompany our old people to the
grave. They've forgotten what it was like to be young. And
how do we know what we'll be like when we're their age?"

Most grandmothers work at lace-making or crocheting
or mending, often gathering in twos or threes in their doorways, talking and working, though the work brings in little
money. It helps pass the time, they say deprecatingly. In
winter and at mealtimes, they are inside keeping the fire
going. Every farmhouse is incomplete without a built-in

grandmother, a large black silhouette in long, full black skirt, black blouse, and shawl bent over the fire from a low, rush-seated wooden chair, feeding the slow flames brittle twigs of pruned grapevines, one by one, or watching the pot of cabbage and potatoes boiling, or grilling the meat. A fire keeps you company, they say. The room smells of wood smoke, cabbage, and broiled meat, and the hot air mixes with the sharp, clear cold from outside that strikes the nostrils like a dash of spring water.

Old women who can no longer do anything at all simply sit, waiting, in the house. Sara told me of one of her old aunts who refused to wait seated. She went to bed and informed her family she would stay there until she died. It took her five years to die, but she stuck to her word, even though the village doctor insisted there was nothing wrong with her and begged, cajoled, and commanded her to get up through all five years.

The grandfathers do whatever work they can. Grandfather Solé went to the fields as long as he was able, even if only to gather and bundle the grape cuttings for the fire. Old Alfonso Miret still putters on his land. At eighty-six, he is bent at the waist parallel to the ground like a windswept tree. From eighty years of bending over it, his face is permanently fixed upon it, and he walks supporting his forward half with a stick as gnarled as his hands and his body, gnarled and twisted out over the land by years of toil. Because he has worked most of his waking hours all his life, the position he has to maintain with a cane while walking becomes natural when he works, and he puts his cane aside to dig the ground or repair a stone wall.

When the old men are unable to work, they do nothing at all. They sit. Perhaps to sit doing nothing for hours is possible only after a day or a lifetime of hard, physical labor. They sit at the café or on a bench in the little square by the church, in a row, saying almost nothing, and doing nothing at all, not even brushing away the flies. Others sit by themselves in the doorway or under a tree in the shade, always on a straight chair or a stone. When the sun sets, they sit by the fire, waiting for the evening meal.

When Tía María fell sick, Raimondo no longer sat among his cronies in the square. Within a month I heard he had moved to Riera, to the house of his son, who worked in a factory. Tía María was in the hospital, soon to return to him, not cured, but able to live out what little time remained at home. No one would stay in a hospital longer than necessary or ever die anywhere but at home, if possible.

A few weeks passed before I went to see Raimondo and María in Riera. I located the house with some difficulty because no one in the village was sure of the number or even the street name. It was one of the many narrow streets that look alike with their rows of green slatted shades draped over rows of iron balconies, and the huge doors opening on identical entrances—small, high-ceilinged, with an overhead lantern in the center and a shabby stone stairway to one side. Several families usually lived in each house. I groped in the dark stairway until I found Raimondo's son's name beside a doorbell on the second-floor landing. I rang repeatedly. At last the door swung back slowly, and I saw the hunched figure of Raimondo, sitting in a dim hallway. Tía María, who had opened the door, greeted me and called to him, "Raimondo, here's the Señora come to visit!"

Raimondo raised his head. His face looked like a curtain fallen on the floor. Where the seams and folds had a pattern before, they had suddenly deepened and crisscrossed, humped and burrowed in a startling way as if the natural pattern of aging had been abruptly disturbed. What had been firm had collapsed, what had been a wrinkle was a deep gash like a wound, and the sparkling blue eyes were faded, rheumy, and vague. He did not move when I came

111

in. When I spoke, he turned gradually, only at his wife's nudging, and stared blankly, without interest, until she told him again who I was.

Tía María had called Concepción, the daughter-in-law, who bustled in, wiping her hands on her apron, her large green eyes greedily authoritative. No sooner had she greeted me than she insisted on showing me the house as if I were there to inspect the dwelling and pass on it. María and Raimondo remained in the entrance hall while I was propelled down a narrow corridor that led past a kitchen—where a motionless figure in black sat near the fire—a dining room, and a series of bedrooms, most with no outside windows. It ended in a minuscule terrace, crowded with wash hanging on lines.

Concepción talked throughout in a loud voice that vibrated in my ears like an insistent alarm.

"It isn't as though there were money to spare," she was saying. "We're poor people. My husband was sick for three years, couldn't work at all. What little we had saved all went then, and what we saved since has gone now on fixing things up for *them.* What can you do? I don't regret it. That's the way it is. But when I hear them say they'll go back to their own house in a month or two . . . after all we've done! They can't go back, you can see that. The doctor forbade María to do any work, and Raimondo has collapsed now he no longer has her to do everything for him. They can't live there alone, and I can't do more than I am now."

When I turned away from the tiny terrace to go back to join Raimondo and Tía María, Concepción planted herself in front of me, blocking the narrow corridor.

"Put yourself in my place!" Her green eyes challenged me. "What else can I do? I have five children, there's my own mother, you saw her in the kitchen, she's eighty-three, and like a child, too—we all get like children when we're old. I can't go up to Las Casas to clean up for them. I've enough work here. Besides, I can't ever leave the house because of Mother. It's all I can manage to get out to buy what's needed."

"Couldn't they get someone in Las Casas to come in and take care of things, *pay* someone?" I asked.

"That costs money," she said.

I thought of Alfonso Miret's paper, of dark stories of relatives stopping at nothing to inherit intact a few pitiable relics—a mahogany bedstead, a miserable acre or two, a tumbledown house.

"Just put yourself in my place," Concepción's voice insisted. "We've sacrificed all we can. I'm not sorry. They're his parents and you have to take care of old people. They're like children, they don't realize. They haven't long to live and they think they're going back home soon." She sniffed in contempt. "They just don't realize how well off they are. They have good food, nothing to do, and a room to themselves. Like children. You can see for yourself!"

She turned to open a door on the corridor and pushed me inside. The room was freshly painted bright pink. The two narrow beds almost touched each other, and there was just enough space on one side to open the shiny new wardrobe, and on the other to adjust the casement window, which looked out on a wall across the street. The only other furniture was a chair and a night table. I recognized Raimondo's battered old radio, on which he used to listen to Soviet shortwave broadcasts in Catalan, once the only broadcasts in that language he could get. "What do you think of communism?" I once asked him. "It'll never work," he said. "And why?" "Because to give to the have-nots, you have to take from the haves, and they'll never agree to it," he answered.

In the closed room the dampness of the tile floors seeped up, spreading through the pink walls in dark blotches, making the layer of paint peel though the walls had just been painted, and at great cost, the daughter-in-law assured me.

Tired of waiting, Raimondo and María had joined us in the bedroom and stood silently beside us. The new wardrobe was expensive, too, Concepción said. "And it's a room with a window. We did everything we could, everything!"

Back home in Las Casas, Raimondo's house was high on the side of a hill, pressed against its neighbor houses for comfort and warmth, with the back terrace hung with little ripe tomatoes for winter, strings of garlic and onions and sausages in the attic, and Raimondo's famous partridges in cages, though he hadn't hunted in over a year now. Neighbors threw scraps to Tía María's large white cat occasionally. It mewed mournfully at times, and at others sunned itself contentedly on the geranium-lined terrace overhanging the now-empty wire enclosures. There, chickens, hens, and rabbits once grew fat for the table, neatly covered with bright green linoleum, under a three-globed overhanging lamp of pale-pink fluted glass, next to the gleaming dark buffet, pride of the house and occupying most of the room, where china and glasses were displayed on rounds of lace made by María in the long winter nights. The sun lit the house from the first rays till the shadows of the hills stretched down the green, terraced valley to guide the grazing goats home for the night.

I stared at the pink walls of the tiny room in which Concepción's voice echoed. The old people watched in silence. I could read no expression on their faces. Attention, nothing more. I left without talking to them.

7 &

Mule in the Well

ONE SUNNY February day when the almonds were in full
blossom, pink and white, a weird clamor and clanging called
me to the window. Looking out, I saw a peasant cart with
the canvas hood up, the back and sides draped with clat-
tering pots and pans, and the mule that drew it wearing a
cockeyed straw hat dangling long, red ribbons. Old, torn
mattresses hung out the back of the cart. Jumping on and
off them, cavorting around the cart in tattered clothes,
beating on frying pans to attract attention, were Paco, the
baker, and the barber. A crowd of children followed, giggling and imitating. Stopping four doors up the street, Paco
pulled a short ladder with half the rungs missing out of the
cart. Slipping and falling as he propped it against the wall
of a corral, clowning as he pretended to run up it without
noticing the missing rungs, he called back over his shoulder
that he was about to get himself a nice fat chicken for
supper.

Just as his head reached the top of the wall, a broom
handle flashed from a window of the house adjoining the
corral and smashed down on the wall, barely missing him.

The woman in the window shrieked, then burst out laughing, scolding Paco as a fool in danger of being beaten as a chicken thief by mistake. Joining in the carnival spirit, she demanded the price of the broken broom in mock anger, while Paco insisted he would pay her by telling her fortune. To the wild giggles of the children and bystanders below, he began to predict the birth of six more children and other preposterous future events.

Later that same February afternoon, when I set out for a walk, I came across Paco and his companions cooking a dish of rice and meat and drinking wine in the fields. I refused the offer to share, but congratulated them on the aroma and on the afternoon's performance. Ah, they smiled, there's only us left now to play jokes at carnival time, everybody else is so serious or so busy earning a living, but you should have seen carnival here ten years ago. All the men in the village took the day off, playing pranks and tricks, and then all of us men cooked an enormous meal together in the café and had a feast.

"I remember one feast," Paco said, "when we drank over a bottle of champagne apiece after all the wine we had for dinner, and nobody remembers how much cognac. I felt so jolly when I went to bed that, though it was almost dawn, there was no use trying to sleep. I was wide awake. So I got up, put on old clothes, took the heaviest hoe in the shed, and went out to the fields. There was enough light to see by when I got there. I worked three hours, hard, sweating, breaking land for planting, came home, had something to eat, went back to bed, and slept till five in the afternoon. Afterwards, the other men told me they'd taken cold showers and I don't know what all, but I woke up feeling fine, just fine."

The following afternoon, when I set off at my usual hour for a long walk through the fields and pine forests, at the bewitching hour when low shadows stretch lazily over gold-tipped wheat fields, Amalia said, "Don't go for a walk today, Señora. There's a strange man in the fields." There were strangers about from time to time, I answered, but I had never had any reason to fear them. "This one is crazy, I think," she said. "He hides behind bushes and jumps out suddenly with a white turban on his head and enormous, staring eyes!" What nonsense, I said, and have you seen him? "Oh no, I'm glad to say I haven't. I'd be frightened out of my wits if I did. But other people have." She was breathless with the pleasurable excitement of fear, like children who invent ghosts to enjoy the tingling shivers the thought gives them.

As I passed the Solés' doorway, José, who was rewinding a frayed rope, looked appreciatively at the sky. "It's a fine afternoon for taking a walk and not getting anywhere," he said. It was, I agreed. Then I thought to ask him if he had heard the report of a strange man around the village.

"A white turban?" José laughed. "Women are like children. If they see a little snake, they think it's a cobra, and if they see a white rock, they think it's an elephant."

"Maybe it's a carnival prank," Paco said, "or just a joke."

"Could be," José conceded. "We used to play jokes like that, hiding and scaring people from other villages when we walked through the mountains at night coming home from a fiesta in some other town."

I did not see the turbaned stranger, but there were other reports of him during the following days. There were signs of someone having made a fire and cooked a meal in one of the stone tool houses near the village. One day Paco saw the man from a distance and had to admit that he did, indeed, act odd and wear a white turban.

At last, when Sara refused to go out alone to gather greens for the goats and the women claimed they only felt

117

safe coming and going from the village laundry vats in groups, José felt obliged to act. One afternoon when Amalia's oldest daughter came running down the street claiming to have seen the turbaned mystery man near the *torrente,* José went to find him. To his great surprise, there was, indeed, a strange man near the *torrente,* wearing an enormous white bandage wrapped round and round his head like a turban. The man was just unwrapping and rewrapping it when José came up; he could see there was nothing wrong with the man's head at all.

"I recognized him," José said when he came back. "He's the brother of a man who sells chickens in Riera. He was born a little odd and wanders off for weeks, then goes back home. Didn't make much sense when he talked to me, but he was perfectly civil."

"He should be reported to the Guardia Civil," Sara said. "He shouldn't be allowed to go around loose frightening women and children." The other women and some of the men were of the same opinion.

José snorted. "You women and children frighten yourselves. How can we report him to the Guardia Civil when he hasn't done anything and, so far as anybody knows, is completely harmless? He has a right to live, too, and to walk wherever he wants to. Nobody's going to report him or bother him, and you silly women will have to stop being afraid of your own shadows. He'll probably go back home in a few days as he always does."

José's tolerance prevailed. As he predicted, the man soon went back to his family without having harmed a soul. "Only cowards act out of fear," José remarked.

A few months later, I had another occasion to appreciate José's tolerance. One afternoon, José hailed me as I set off on my usual walk. "I have to put a pail of water on some newly planted cabbages. Want to come along?" he asked.

I knew he meant exactly what he said because I had seen him do it before. He would draw a single pail of water from the well next to his vegetable plot, set the pail on the ground, and use a small tin can to distribute the contents of the pail evenly among thirty cabbages.

In June, the peasants' hardest month, most men stay in the fields until the long shadows turn to night, until they can't see to work anymore, especially the older men who know no way to keep making ends meet except to work harder, longer. A number of them, like old Alfonso Miret, can no longer stand up straight after a lifetime of such labor. It is as if they had been deliberately stunted to make the land produce, just as the tortuous olive trees lining the road are deliberately stunted to make them produce more fruit.

On the way to José's vegetable patch, we passed a field newly plowed by tractor. It had been an old vineyard, too old to yield well. José shook his head, saying he would never have plowed it now, under the new moon, because the roots would grow back, while under the old moon, they would die. People didn't pay attention to the moon the way they used to, he added, though the moon should really be taken into account more than it was. For instance, if you made a well at the time of the new moon, all the water would run out, while under the old moon, it would hold.

"No one knows why this is so, but it is," José said. "And if you dig up the old vines at the time of the new moon, ten years later you'll still be unable to plant that field for the roots of vines that keep sprouting there. The young don't listen to the old wisdom now, though it's been proven by generation after generation. Yet, perhaps they're right. As Paco says, if you tractor the land, you dig so deep the grape stumps are dug out anyway and it doesn't matter whether they're dead or not. Everything's so new now, the old ways don't always count."

We had reached José's well, which stood in the middle of the vegetable patch. The plants were neatly, almost artistically arranged and carefully planned, in contrast to the rather haphazard plot nearby that belonged to a peasant in the next town. As we approached, my dog ran sniffing to the well, where he began barking. "That's odd," José muttered, walking over. "*Caramba!* That's no joke!" he exclaimed. "There's a dead mule in there!"

"It fell in?" I asked incredulously.

"Couldn't have, couldn't fall in backwards, and wouldn't anyway . . . too narrow." The well was deep, some twenty feet deep, but no more than two feet in diameter.

José was silent a minute. "Someone had to put it there . . . I think I know who. I think it's a present from my neighbor." He pointed at the scraggly vegetable patch next to his own. "If I'm right, it's not ill will, just ignorance. He's a little stupid, that man, and lazy too. Probably just wanted to save the trouble of burying it." He peered down at the motionless brown body. "Well, he'll have to bury it, get it out and bury it. And we'll just say nothing about it," he added, "because people might get in a panic over it and there's no need. We'll check the water out in Riera to make sure it's all right," he filled a small flask he kept in his tool hut as he spoke, "and say nothing to anyone if it is."

I offered to take him by car right away, and we left for Riera. I waited quite a while in the car, where we had agreed to meet. I was not surprised José was late. Punctuality is not one of the local virtues. In a country where even the railroad station clock may be an hour or two off, hardly anyone knows what time it is, or cares very much.

When José appeared, he was very excited. "The water?" I asked at once. "Water's fine," he said. That was not what had aroused him. "I was late talking about the *nens* in Barcelona," he said, referring to the human towers I had heard of, but never seen. *Nens* is Catalan for children, but *the nens* are amateur acrobats, traditionally stone masons, who specialize in making human towers at fiestas. The origin of this custom is obscure, its practice limited to a handful of towns near Barcelona, but its fame is such that competitions are held in Barcelona itself and reported in detail in all the newspapers. Participants and devotees like José can spend hours discussing and criticizing performances and the respective strengths and weaknesses of groups from the various towns. Two of the best would be in Barcelona to compete at the festival of San Juan the following Thursday, José explained excitedly.

Curious to see this event, I suggested we drive to Barcelona together. The car was quickly filled. I invited Grandmother Solé as a matter of form, though certain she would refuse. "Ay no," she said, "I wouldn't go there, so far away. Men are loco, all loco." Paco wanted to go, which meant Sara had to stay. Rosetta decided to come too, in order to visit Carmen and see her new apartment.

No one knew what time the competition was supposed to start, but José was so nervous about the possibility of missing it, and so eager to see all the preparations and talk to the people participating in it, that we left very early in the morning, so early that no one was up but the rich peasant Malla, bundling hay.

"It'll rot the way he's doing it," José said. "Works harder than anybody, but harvests less. He never learned anything about farming and never will, but nobody can tell him anything."

There were signs of the festival everywhere in Barcelona, in decorations, in preparations for fireworks, and in occasional glimpses down sidestreets of the huge papier-mâché figures of Isabella and Ferdinand, who preside over every local festival with their shiny pink faces and smug expressions. Beneath their long velvet robes peep the dusty shoes of the men who support them and twirl them about to the reedy notes of the *tenora,* a kind of cross between trumpet and oboe. We left José and Paco in the square where the *nens* were already gathering, dressed in red shirts, white trousers with red wool sashes wrapped round and round their waists, and red cotton bandannas tied on their heads. Rosetta and I continued across Barcelona to visit Carmen.

Her apartment was in the Gothic quarter of Barcelona, down a dank medieval street and up a dank medieval staircase, humid and close-smelling as a cave. Carmen answered the door. Eagerly she poured out news of people she had met, things she had seen and done, plans for an excursion to Lourdes during her three-week August vacation. The apartment's faded lace curtains and stained, satin-covered chairs bore mute witness to the genteel poverty of the landlady, reduced to letting rooms with kitchen privileges. "How splendid everything is," Rosetta said, "how rich it looks."

Carmen's eyes betrayed nothing of what she thought, though they were as honest as they had been when I first knew her as a plump, freckled village girl of sixteen. She herself was as candid as she had been then, but her reactions were often mixed, her enthusiasms tempered. She had learned the city was not only a place of a thousand opportunities, but noisy, dirty, agitated; that its inhabitants were not all sophisticated and happy. She contrasted the strained faces and short tempers of Barcelonians with the relaxed, smiling countenances of the villagers. But she would not think of living anywhere except in Barcelona, she hastened to emphasize, because with all its faults it was a marvelous place to be, to be young in, and to see the world from.

We set out to see her world, her place of work, her school, the nearby market, and the cheap workman's restaurant where she and her friends splurged on dinner on a rare occasion. When we at last joined José and Paco in the square, they had been standing, watching the competition in the hot sun for three hours.

Every time one of the groups of *nens* made a new tower, it would take a half-hour for them to get the first ring in position, as if they had never done anything of the sort before and had to decide from the very beginning how to go about it. Through most of the wait, you could see nothing over the heads of the crowd pressing closely in the hot June sun, or if you saw anything, it was only a knot of red-shirted men disputing and waving their arms. José, as close as he could get to the *nens* and talking volubly to the enthusiasts surrounding them, had the face of a six-year-old on Christmas morning.

Once the bottom circle of the sturdiest, stockiest men is in place, arms interlocked at shoulder height, the tower rises quickly and harmoniously to the triumphant music of *tenora* and drum. Other men, almost as stocky, climb up onto the shoulders of the first by digging bare feet into the red cummerbunds for a toehold. Soon there are five tiers of four men each, the bottom two rings supported by the outstretched hands and arms of the public, who press closely around the human tower.

Nevertheless, the tower begins to shake. The faces of the men at the bottom are flattened with strain. The quivering of their muscles grows into a more and more pronounced trembling; their bodies and arms shake uncontrollably. As the tremor spreads upward, the tower begins to sway dangerously, but two young boys nevertheless scramble up it, their feet seeking toeholds from sash to shoulder to sash. When they are well on the way, one more starts up, even younger, perhaps six or seven. A boy of five, destined for the top, is resisting with tears and terror. The boy is the key to the tower's success, because if he does not get to the top, squat on the heads of the last ring, and raise one arm in the air before the tower collapses, the whole effort is a failure. Someone always promises him a bicycle if he will climb up, José told us afterward. Up he goes with the help of an occasional hand unclasped to push him on his way. Quickly he crosses over the shoulders of the top two boys and, half doubled up, lifts his hand briefly in the air to the applause of the crowd and a final roll of the drums. The tower is a success even if it should collapse now, folding down upon itself like shuffled cards falling into place, the men on the bottom row and the enthusiasts around them forming a bed of locked arms and bowed heads ready to receive falling bodies. This time the tower is disassembled level by level to continuing applause. The little boy is praised and petted, but does not get his bicycle. It seems, though they always promise him one, they never give it to him.

Paco shortly drifted off to the shade of a nearby bar. Because José was too absorbed even to tell us when he might want to leave, we arranged to meet when it was all over in the bar Paco had chosen. In the meantime, Rosetta, Carmen, and I wandered over to the cathedral to see the *sardanas,* the traditional dance of Catalonia.

In the square in front of the cathedral, just as in the square of the smallest Catalan town, anyone can join the ever-widening circles that form spontaneously in response to the first piercing notes of *sardana* music, as if those notes were pebbles cast in a pool, forming spreading rings. Men and women, young and old, detach themselves from the crowd in silence as if carefully rehearsed and form circle within circle, circle beside circle, filling all the empty space of the public square, hands joined, arms raised, feet moving to the music. The arms are immobile. The bodies move in unison right or left, always upright, sedate; the feet crisscross back and forth in a complicated pattern, lightly, rapidly, then halt as the music is abruptly interrupted by another announcement of the *tenora*. A sustained note precedes a renewal of the music, with a new pattern for the feet. The faces are solemn, concentrated. Everyone has to count to follow the pattern, dictated for each circle by one silently and spontaneously chosen leader. All the while, more circles continue to form, and those formed continue to enlarge.

In the *sardana*, you feel the same spirit of spontaneous cooperation that you see in the building of human towers, in the rhythm of the harvest, in all the old harmonious ways of living, working, and celebrating together. The *sardana*, I thought as I watched, reflects the essence of these people, villager or Barcelonian.

As people join in, hands parts and reclasp to include the newcomers, whoever they may be. The purses and packages they carry are tossed in a growing heap in the center of the circle. Carmen, who had joined them, blended and belonged.

"She belongs in Barcelona," Rosetta said, echoing my thought. "I see it now, she belongs here."

8 ❧

A Wedding

When Josefina turned fourteen, she left school but she did not follow Carmen to Barcelona, though she insisted she was not going to marry a peasant and settle in Las Casas. She seemed happy in a restless way, working beside her mother during the day, giggling for hours with the village girls of her age in the evening, and going with them to fiestas in neighboring towns or to the movies in Riera on Sundays. Bus service to Riera had increased since our arrival from once a week on market days to several times a day in order to accommodate the growing number of immigrant laborers from the south who commuted between Riera's expanding factories and the cheaper housing in Las Casas. On Sundays the bus made one round trip bearing half Las Casas, laborer and peasant, to town for the afternoon. Riera's three movie houses were filled from 4:00 P.M. until 8:00, when there was an outpouring of people to the cafés and the Ramblas, always the noisiest, most crowded, and most sought-after part of town.

In Riera, as elsewhere in Spain, the Ramblas is a broad, paved island several blocks long, flanked by two wide streets that channel most of the town's vehicular traffic up one side and down the other. Cafés line the pedestrian island on either side, but the center is open for strollers, who walk up and down it for hours. With honking cars on two sides and an endless parade of people in the middle, the Ramblas offers the Spaniard two of the things he appreciates most, noise and crowds. It is here you find the pretentious villas with double staircases swooping into rose gardens, built on money from wine shipped to South America or the sugar trade with Cuba before Spain lost its Latin American colonies a century and a half ago.

Every evening and every Sunday afternoon, unless it rains, the Ramblas is filled with families, baby carriages, and engaged couples, but it is particularly designed for the unmarried. This is the place where boy meets girl, chaperoned by half the population of the town. On Sundays Josefina and her giggling friends were among the groups of unengaged girls who walked arm in arm, round and round the Ramblas, up one side and down the other, passing on each round, face to face, and looking over, groups of boys walking in the opposite direction. It was here that sixteen-year-old Josefina caught the eye of the town carpenter's oldest son, and here the pair exchanged glances for weeks, then a few sentences for months, and at last walked around the Ramblas hand in hand, whereupon the carpenter's son had to declare his honorable intentions promptly.

The morning after the engagement became official, I had occasion to call on the town carpenter about some work. When he was not in his shop, I knew to look for him in the wine shop next door. If he was not hunting for wild asparagus or fishing for mussels, Salvador was usually doing errands for someone or helping to solve a problem. Because people were always calling on him for help or advice, and because his shop was too noisy to talk in, he spent most of his time in the wine shop next door. It was there I would consult him when I had to select a gift for a wedding or a First Communion, or to repay someone who had done us a favor. So many people did things for us without pay: the garageman insisted he mended tires out of friendship, the local doctor refused to consider our visits as other than social, the peasant who cleaned out our septic tank in an emergency refused compensation on the grounds it was a job no one would undertake for money. In each case, finding a suitable present required knowing local tastes and standards of value. Salvador was an invaluable counselor. Always glad to have an excuse to stay away from his shop, he would drop whatever he was doing and, after a long discussion in the comparative quiet of the bar, patiently accompany me around town, ready to spend half the day if necessary to find the right gift. From him I learned that it was the box that counted, not the candy, that the most magnificent flowers were inappropriate in a country where, despite occasional frost or snow, some plants were always in bloom, and that the garage mechanic would appreciate a handful of ninety-cent cigars more than boxes of the ones he smoked every day.

"Not here!" Salvador's sons called out cheerily when I poked my head in the carpentry shop.

A gnome-sized half-door, cut into the heavy carriage door, opens into the wine shop, where the scarred wooden tables and chairs, and the barrels of wine, sherry, manzanilla, and cognac that line the walls are all steeped in a somber sepia light, recalling the yellowed, brown-ink engravings you might find in an old private library. Overlooking the scene are the casement windows of the owner's kitchen, reached by a crooked dark staircase leading from the bar. The town carpenter was there with five of his friends eating fried baby octopus and drinking local champagne to celebrate his son's engagement. The old man specialized in time-consuming, tedious jobs of repair and restoration, but for the past ten years he had finished none of them. "I can't," he confessed. "There's no point. I'd be ashamed to charge today's prices for the time it takes."

Engagement or none, he was usually to be found in this bar or another, lost in dreams of the life he would like to live, leaving the present, with its ever-looming stacks of lumber and roaring machines, to his workmen and two ambitious sons. For the past three years, because of Riera's rapid expansion, his shop has been filled with new raw lumber being slapped into doors and windows for new houses, always hurriedly, with the masons demanding more production, faster, and issuing new orders that will never be filled on time. If he had money enough to live on, Salvador once told me, he would still work at his trade, but not filling orders. Instead, he would make something he wanted to make, a table or a chair, in his own way, on his own time, and give it to someone he liked.

"Have a glass of champagne," he said when I came in to talk to him. It was only 8:30 in the morning, I protested, but he pressed a glass in my hand, saying, "You have to know how to seize the good moments, the bad ones come by themselves."

"And when will the wedding be?" I asked.

"Oh, not for years," he answered airily. "First Rafael has to do his military service—that's a year to eighteen months, and then they'll have to get an apartment and furnish it with everything under the sun, whether they'll ever use it all or not. My wife has hand-embroidered sheets and towels we've never unfolded and cupboards full of glasses that are only for dusting, too good to use. Nowadays, young couples still have to have all the old things, but they're also buying refrigerators and gas stoves and heaters, so they're either middle-aged by the time they marry or else buried in debt." He laughed, pouring more champagne. "Let them do what they want. Life's for young people. We old ones can't keep up."

When the wedding took place, a conservative three years later, I was invited along with some forty or fifty people from Las Casas, Riera, and outlying villages where one family or the other had relatives or friends. The ceremony was to take place at Montserrat, the sacred monastery west of Barcelona that houses the patron of Catalonia, the Black Madonna, whose face has been darkened over centuries by smoke from lamps and candles lit by the faithful. Said to have been made by Saint Luke and brought to Spain by Saint Peter, the Madonna was buried in 717 during the Moorish invasion and rediscovered by passing shepherds a century and a half later, about the time the monastery was built. In the Middle Ages the Germans believed they would find the Holy Grail on the saw-toothed peaks of Montserrat. Present-day Catalans believe they will find the perfect marriage there. For that reason the monastery has become a sort of marriage factory, organized to accommodate thousands of couples holding weddings there every year, just as it has organized to accommodate hundreds of daily visitors and to provide them with every adjunct of tourism from souvenir and postcard shops to restaurants, guided tours, well-labeled walks to hermit shrines, admission fees, and cable cars to get up the mountain of Montserrat that pilgrims used to climb so tediously.

For many from Las Casas who went to the wedding, the most impressive part of the expedition was the bus Paco and Sara hired to transport their guests. Modern vehicles were still novel enough to hold great fascination. I remember once driving to the Barcelona airport with our maid,

Amalia, who had come along to see what an airport looked like. We took a magnificent road through rugged pine-covered mountains with ruined castles high on the peaks of jagged red rocks. Depressed by the loneliness of the landscape, she kept sighing and repeating, "How sad!" However, she recovered her spirits at the airport and spent a two-hour wait happily seated on a bench in front of the main door, muscular arms folded majestically, watching with intense satisfaction the arrival and departure of shiny, modern buses filled with people.

"What a beautiful bus it was!" mused one woman the day after Josefina's wedding. "It shone like the moon, all silvery, and inside there were huge windows and the most comfortable, softest seats you ever sat in." I thought of the tiny windows and rigid straight chairs in the villagers' houses. Is it any wonder everyone liked the bus and sat in it patiently while it rounded up guests in various towns and villages before taking the long, winding road to Montserrat? "What a strong bus!" the woman added. "When you got in, it didn't sink a bit. It flew around corners and down hills." They were used to feeling a cart or small car sink as they got in, these stout women who weighed almost as much as their men. They were then just beginning to think that perhaps they weighed too much, an idea that gained currency after the arrival of tourists, foreign women who remained slim and active into their thirties and forties. I will always remember the bus driver looking at a snapshot of a slender young Frenchwoman in a bikini as he sighed and remarked, "*My* wife looks like a herring on a grill."

The women all crossed themselves as the motor started and muttered Hail Marys as the bus roared down the road while carts and pedestrians got out of the way as best they could. Some of the women were squealing and laughing with delight like children on a roller coaster. Others were beginning to disagree about which windows should be open and which should be shut, an argument Paco settled by having everyone sing. They sang all the way to Montserrat, a few hours' drive, and all the way back. There were many hoarse voices in Las Casas for several days.

Between notes of music, they ate. A wedding dinner was scheduled to follow the ceremony, but no one was going to set out on such a long journey into the unknown without a good sack of provisions from home. There were baskets with wine, bread, sausages, tomatoes, ham, and even small pots of stew, roasted rabbit, and fried fish. One woman was dissuaded with difficulty from bringing along a couple of live chickens, just in case. The bus had to stop several times to let out some of the children, upset by the combination of excitement, overeating, and the unaccustomed motion of the bus. "That's natural," the villagers said as the bus started up again, the women crossing themselves, and Paco leading them all in song.

Everything along the way was noted with keen interest. The men commented on the quality of the soil, the manner of pruning fruit trees (which varies from one valley to the next), the type of vine, and the productiveness of the vineyards. The women commented on the towns, comparing the facilities, streets, and cleanliness with those of their own. "How white it is! Ours should look like that. They must whitewash every year! And the backs as well as the fronts!" "How nice and flat, how easy to walk in. A flat town is better." "They must have lots of water, look at all the flowerpots in the windows." But what aroused the most comment was any kind of river. The smallest trickle excited more attention than the jagged peaks for which Montserrat is named, rising spectacularly out of the plain like fingers pointing at the sky, clearly visible for a hundred miles or more.

Our arrival at the foot of Montserrat set off another flurry of excitement, akin to panic, when the women saw the cable cars that carry all visitors to the top, a trip made on foot or by mule in the old days. "Aiee, no," they squealed, "I'm not getting in one of those, I'm staying on the ground right here! Look at it sway—it's going to drop right down. Aiee, no!" Paco took charge with his usual competence, dividing the flock into several groups to go up in several cars, and putting stout-hearted leaders in each group to encourage the rest. Nevertheless, when the time came, a few had to be pushed in, calling on all the saints, resisting, but at the same time reluctant to be left behind alone. When Grandmother Solé heard about the cable cars, she regretted less having had to stay home to nurse José, who had come down with one of his frequent attacks of grippe. "I would have missed the wedding anyway," she said, "because I would never have gone up in one of those things."

Once the villagers were in the cable car, the danger became a real one. Relaxed and hugely diverted by the novelty and splendid view of treetops, they began pointing out things to each other and calling each other from side to side. "Look, look!" Sara would call from the left, "You can see the roof of a house down there!" And everyone would run to her side of the cable car. Since almost everyone weighed close to 180 pounds, the cable car lurched and dangled furiously at the onrush, at which everyone raced back to the right, causing an equally dangerous surge of weight. The ticket taker became frantic, anticipating disaster. Frightened children sobbed, and the women, once again timid, stood still, crossing themselves.

When they staggered out of the cable cars with relief, the distractions at the top of Montserrat made them forget the panic of the past ten minutes. They seemed to find the hotels, restaurants, souvenir shops, and blatant commercialism surrounding the ancient monastery and cathedral as novel and intriguing as the historic monuments themselves. Paco had a time keeping them together. They were inside shops fingering shiny souvenirs of the famous peaks to be seen outside; they were disappearing down sidestreets, hanging back, running ahead, and enjoying themselves enormously. There was just time before the ceremony for a brief walk down one of the many paths leading to shrines, ancient hermitages, and grottoes, opening on spectacular views of the plain and the Pyrenees, distant Barcelona, and the sea. You can see the island of Mallorca on a very clear day, we were told. We also filed through the gray-walled cathedral, past the hallowed shrine in the apse where the Virgin of Montserrat was on display.

Inside other, newer gray walls, flanking the approach to the cathedral, was a complete setup for weddings. Our wedding party, including bride and groom with their suitcases, filed upstairs past rooms in which we could see the photographers on permanent duty taking wedding portraits of other brides and grooms. At the end of the corridor was a series of dressing rooms. I joined the women in the room assigned the bride, a room large enough to accommodate all of us. There the bride was arrayed in white satin with the traditional white lace mantilla, while the mothers of the young couple put on high combs and black lace mantillas. Rafael and Josefina then waited for the photographer in a corridor with other couples about to be wed. After being photographed, the couples lined up again at the entrance to the chapel, each surrounded by its own wedding party. Ceremony succeeded ceremony in the chapel all day in a good season, for Montserrat brings luck to the newly christened as well as the newly wed. Many Catalans, and now many of the Estremeñans and Andalusians who migrate from the south to Catalonia, name their children Montserrat.

The service over, we all congratulated Rafael and Josefina and trooped to one of the numerous banquet halls, where ten large tables were already occupied by other wedding parties, each presided over by a bride and groom. Toasts, jokes, and innuendos rang from tables all around as the Spanish champagne flowed and course followed course until no one could eat or drink anything more. Everyone ate a great deal out of respect for the host, but private comments afterward were highly critical. Although tolerant of gimcrackery and commercialism, perhaps because such things are so foreign to them, the villagers are not easy customers in a restaurant. They are used to the best of olive oils, the purest of wines, the freshest of vegetables and meats, cooked at home, with no waiting between courses. While delays annoy them, pretension and display arouse their contempt; cobwebbed bottles, crystal cruets, and elaborate garnishes do not deceive them. "The oil wasn't pure," "The wine wasn't natural," "The foods were so mixed up you couldn't tell what you were eating" . . . so the three-hour banquet was dismissed, though everyone had a good time.

At last it was the hour to leave, by cable car, of course. "Aiee, you're not getting me in that thing again," declared one of the fatter, more timid women, sitting down on a stone. Persuasion, tugging, protest, threats—nothing worked until at last every member of the party got on the cable cars and left her to the greater fear of being alone, which drove her to squeeze in the door of the last car to pray frantically and cross herself over and over all the way down.

The bride and groom, who had changed into traveling clothes in the Montserrat dressing rooms, were dispatched with their suitcases to Barcelona for a three-day honeymoon, while the guests climbed back in the chartered bus to sing all the way home. Sara cried throughout the trip to think her daughter would now be living in Riera instead of at home. The wedding party reached Las Casas late, exhausted, and fully satisfied, most exclaiming how good it was to be home again, and that all one had to do was leave for a short time to know how good it was.

9 ॐ

Death

WHEN A villager dies, the church bell tolls. When it tolls at night, one awakens and wonders. Is it the baker's father? Haven't seen him sitting on the hill under the pine tree in at least a week. Is it the newborn baby that caught pneumonia? The mason, who is nearing eighty, yet scampers over rooftops younger men fear? "I'll go," he'd always volunteer if others hesitated. I used to watch him in fear. "Don't worry, I'm careful," he would call down to me, "because it's always so sad if an old man dies." Raimondo is now dead, but the bell is not for Tía María, who lives in that tiny room in Riera, closely guarded by the green-eyed daughter-in-law. I visited María from time to time, bringing herbs she liked from the hills. With her small head and brilliant black eyes, she looked more and more like a bird in a cage. I was certain she had enough money to live on her own in her own house, and I knew she longed for the village. Only custom kept her prisoner and only death would bring release, but the tocsin was not for her or for anyone outside the village.

By sunrise the men were harnessing the carts, the

women sweeping back the dust of the street in neat stripes in front of their houses, and everyone knew it was José Solé who had died, carried off suddenly by what had seemed to be only a stubborn grippe. Whenever I passed his doorway now, a vacant frame would remind me of our hours of talk and companionship.

A sudden spatter of raindrops pitted the thick dust of the street. From the somber crowd came the click of umbrellas opening and the stir of people pressing toward sheltering doorways. Grapevines in the surrounding fields bowed before an abrupt sweep of wind. Children laughed with delight, spreading their hands to watch the heavy drops land and roll slowly off. A baby of four months kicked and squirmed in its mother's arms to turn its face up into the rain, protesting vigorously when the mother withdrew into the entrance of the nearest house. With the rest, I pushed my way in.

The mistress of the house, Grandmother Angela, standing in her doorway beside me, held her knitted black shawl to her throat as she looked at the darkening sky and said softly, "Ay, that's how life is."

"Death is always new," said another villager. "No matter how much you expect it, when it comes, it's always new."

"Everybody dies," Grandmother Angela remarked with satisfaction. "Everybody. Rich and poor. All alike."

"No one escapes," said another, and they talked of one old woman who had been terrified of dying; of how she had been afraid and resisted up to the end, but died anyway, just like all the rest.

Grandmother Angela shrugged with contempt. "I'm ready," she said softly, her shoulders bowed by fifteen long years of widowhood and failing sight and limbs. "I'm useless now, no good for anything."

The church bell that had announced the death of José

Solé the night before began to toll again. A young girl retied her hair ribbons while another admired her Sunday dress. Both began giggling. The priest arrived carrying a tall cross, with two choirboys close on his heels, their starched, white, hand-embroidered smocks exposing bare, dusty legs and scuffed sandals. He spoke a brief prayer at the entrance to the Solé house, where the coffin awaited on two upended wine barrels. There was a hollow rumble like the sound of distant drums when the pallbearers lifted the coffin off the barrels.

Behind the coffin with its four pallbearers came the men of the dead man's family, followed by the rest of the village men, all in heavy black wool suits though it was August. Last came the women of the family, the other village women, the children, and a few razor-backed dogs. I fell into file next to the baker's wife, Rosetta. As the procession headed for the church, other villagers, who had waited in their own houses, joined us. One of the women tossed a discouraging stone at the dogs without breaking her pace.

"How happy he is now," Grandmother Angela sighed as she leaned on her cane in the doorway to watch the coffin pass bearing the man who had been her lifetime neighbor, schoolmate, playmate, and friend. She made no move to join the procession. For ten years her rheumatic legs had carried her no farther than his house next door, where she sat knitting or crocheting on fine days with his wife, now his widow, in the arched carriage entrance. When the last of the line had passed, Señora Angela hobbled next door to join the other old women in black who had stayed to console the new widow.

Perhaps she was remembering her own husband's death, fifteen years earlier. He had been a strong, jolly man, who worked every day of his life and many nights without spending a day in bed until one day at the age of sixty-six, when he did not get up. On his deathbed that afternoon, he

141

gathered his family and said, "I'm going to die very soon and when I'm dead and you come back from the cemetery, I want you to take the two fattest chickens and the two fattest rabbits and kill them and eat them because then I'll be content and you'll be content." And so they had done.

From a window down the street, the oldest man in the village, Alfonso Miret, smiled as he waved a good-bye to his friend José. Almost all the rest of the villagers went to the funeral, as they did to anyone's funeral. The village is so small, they explain, there would otherwise never be enough people to escort the dead properly. Besides, most of them are related in one way or another.

The village children enjoy funerals thoroughly, chattering, staring, trotting beside the procession, hovering outside the church door during the service or darting in and out with a complete lack of awe, delighted to have something happen in their uneventful lives. The only one stricken was José Solé's thirteen-year-old grandson, Pepe, walking beside his mother, swollen-eyed and red-faced, so miserable he was barely aware of the interested stares of his playmates. He confided to his mother later that he kept thinking of the cat he had found last harvest time, stretched out beside the vat where the wine was fermenting, its limbs stiff, its rigid jaws drawn back in a snarl. The fumes killed it when it walked over the vat, his father said. Though he knew his grandfather had died of a stroke, not fumes, when he imagined him dead, he saw him with mangy gray fur and a snarl. Too frightened to sleep in the house with the dead man upstairs, he had been taken in by Señora Angela next door the night before.

The way from the church to the cemetery is long and hard, little wider than a cart track and sunk so far in the ground that it must once have been one of the many river beds long gone dry. One's feet do not fit the pair of cart ruts carved five fingers deep into the rocky ground. It had been the main highway to Madrid a few hundred years ago, when cartwheels first began wearing down the stone riverbed, bandits ruled the hills behind the cemetery, and priests carried sword canes for safety.

The woolen-clothed pallbearers perspire, groping for a footing. On either side, grapes hang, ripe, firm, tightly bunched, their skins as clean as a painting of grapes because there has been no rain and mildew to rot them this year. They are small from lack of rain, but sweet. The wine will be strong and good.

The peasants near me were talking of the lack of rain. "It's lucky the storm passed us by," Rosetta said of the brief shower of an hour ago. The mountain wind was stirring the heavy branches of the grapevines, the sky cleared, and sun gilded the leaves. The air had a foretaste of October, when the vines stripped of fruit turn gold, then orange, then deep red brown before leaving the black stalks nude under the winter winds from the Pyrenees, icy blasts hurtling over snow-covered peaks, down the coast to thunder in chimneys.

"It won't be long now," Rosetta said, and I nodded. I had also been thinking of the harvest. Everyone in the village was.

She looked across the fields. "I hear Gorri's son is leaving to work in a factory in Barcelona. Those vineyards are his, and good land, too. That makes five more men that have left since the beginning of the year. If it weren't for people moving in from the south, the village would be half empty. Still, I don't know what will become of the harvest in a few years," Rosetta sighed. "And what about the old people, left alone in their old age?"

I nodded sympathetically. That's when you needed your children in Spain. You took care of them when they were young and they took care of you when you were old. That's the way it is . . . or was. Times had changed.

As for the vineyards, once abandoned, it was unlikely they would ever be vineyards again, though grapes had probably been grown here since the Roman occupation, when Pliny and Martial praised the wine from this coast. It was wine that had made the region rich once, but now wine was making it poor.

"Look at my nephew Alfonso," continued Rosetta. "He's driving a truck. Always liked mechanical things and his parents let him go, though they can't keep up the land by themselves. But then, the young men of today can't do the work their fathers did anyway."

And wouldn't want to, I thought. Middle-aged peasants like Paco Solé were the last of the line. You had only to walk down the village street in the evening around ten, before supper, to see that. It was the middle-aged and old you saw sitting in the freshness of their doorways to cool off, waiting, after the day's harvesting, for a supper of cabbage and potatoes with a charcoal-broiled salt herring, huge slices of crusty bread, and last year's wine, carefully calculated to last until this year's would be ready at Christmas.

"You can't blame them," Rosetta said. "Even the rich are finding land doesn't pay anymore. I've heard the Miros want to sell out."

"What would Paco do then?" I asked. "Isn't a good part of the land he works theirs?"

"Oh, they have to offer it to him first," she answered. "Anyhow, who would buy land up here in the mountains?"

The sun was bright, the sky almost clear. We passed through tall iron gates opening into a square yard enclosed by high walls and planted with four rows of cypress.

"We could make the cemetery look better than this if we took just a little trouble," Rosetta said, looking at the ground so sunbaked in the windless enclosure that it was bare except for tufts of the most tenacious weeds. The walls, lined on three sides of the enclosure with square niches like cupboard drawers, looked weather-stained and neglected despite the wax wreaths of black and deep purple flowers.

An identical wreath adorned the lid of José Solé's coffin, now lying on the ground in the middle of the yard. Four long tapers burned beside it. The priest spoke a few words and left, followed by some of the villagers. Most, however, stayed.

"What are they waiting for?" I asked.

"Now they're going to take out his second son, the one who died in 1946, and people are waiting to see him," Rosetta explained.

The crowd pressed into a huddle. A moment later, I saw in their midst a pair of ankle-high shoes lolling grotesquely large and lifelike on the ground. A parting of the crowd showed them to be attached to the incredibly thin legs of an emaciated corpse. A man's suit hung faded and loose on the shrunken remains. People elbowed each other out of the way to see better. Children pushed through knees and legs to get a look.

"It's a lucky thing the son was dead for more than two years," the woman next to me remarked. "Since you can't take them out for two years by law, if room was needed in the family niche earlier, it'd be too bad. They'd have to get another one."

The conversation she began about niches continued on the way back to the village.

"We ought to get another one for our house," Rosetta said. "We have two in the family, but a lot of people, too. There wouldn't be room for all."

"We don't have room either," another agreed. "Of course, if the dead have been dead a long time, you can get a

145

good number in. There are just a few bones left and you can pile them all together, but when you stop and think —there's my mother and father, my husband's father, an uncle, an aunt, two sisters, an older brother, three cousins, my husband and myself—" she was counting on her fingers —"there certainly isn't room for all of us, and besides, three of them are old now, and any day . . ."

Other people walking alongside began to consider this housing shortage, too, calculating the number of dead already laid away in their niches and how many might be expected to join them in the near future.

"One thing we ought to do," a middle-aged man broke in, "is fix the road to the cemetery since we all have to come this way. But nobody thinks of it till the day it's needed."

As he spoke, I wondered if it was true. For the five hundred or more years the village had existed, almost everyone had been born in it, lived in it, and died in it, growing grapes and making wine. *Es así.* There was no other way to live or work. Children not only worked with their parents, they lived with them all their lives, the sons with their mothers, the daughters moving to their husbands' parents' houses. No old person was left alone until, like José Solé, he had been accompanied by the whole village down that road to the cemetery, where his bones joined those of his family. It was the same in all the villages up and down the coast, through centuries of wars, invasions, foreign occupation, and changes of regime. But now? Nothing the village had been or had known was certain anymore. The land, the stone and mud house, a cart, and a mule were the sum of the worldly goods José Solé was leaving after a life of toil. In the old days it was enough to assure the future of the family. But now? No one knew for certain. The industrial revolution, the technological revolution, and the social revolution were overtaking the countryside all at once, and new was replacing old so fast that towns, land, families, and individuals were sometimes transformed beyond recognition in half a decade. Las Casas del Torrente could no more escape the wave of the future than it could escape from the path of an avalanche. The bell had tolled for José Solé, for his way of life, for all the old ways of Spain.

10 &

The Sea

"MY LIFE is over now," said Grandmother Solé in the house with the other women in black, most of whom had left their houses only to go to church since the death of their husbands. Numb from nursing her husband, always with him in the same room, sharing his bed even at the moment of his death, Grandmother Solé would soon feel the emptiness custom forbids her to fill with distractions. Still, mourning had been much more severe just a short time ago, her daughter-in-law told me. A mere twenty years before, the shutters of the house would be closed after a death in the family and not a ray of light allowed in for a full year. Custom had not yet changed much in the south of Spain, I learned the day after the funeral when I sent Amalia to the Solé house to return a borrowed tool. She came back shocked that Josefina, who had stayed overnight to console her grandmother, had opened the door to the street. "The morning after her grandfather's death!" Amalia exclaimed. "Think of it! To have so little respect for public opinion, so little thought for face. In my land, the family stays in the house. Why, when my uncle died, my aunt stayed in the house for three years, three whole years without stepping out the door, and she wore a black kerchief over her head for eight years, so long that all her hair fell out. That may have been going too far, but to show yourself at the street door the day after!" She shook her head.

"He wasn't very old," said one of José Solé's cronies, sitting in the café at the table where the dwindling group of old men always gathered on Sunday afternoons and evenings. "How old was he anyway?"

"Seventy," one of the men answered, taking from his pocket the printed card distributed at the funeral to ask for prayers for the dead. It had stayed in his suit pocket for the past month since the funeral, and would probably be there two years later, along with cards from baptisms, First Communions, and from other funerals, for he had only one real suit. Since he wore it only for special occasions and Sundays, it hardly ever had to be cleaned.

"Young," the first speaker remarked with a certain satisfaction, having himself reached the superior age of seventy-three. "But that's what often happens with strong men. They go hard all their lives, then suddenly fall apart."

"He had a tough life," another said. "With two sons dead, he and Paco had to work like dogs to keep the land going."

"How will Paco manage alone?" another wondered.

"Oh, he'll manage," said the baker's father, old Alfonso Miret, "with machines and new ways of doing things. I didn't think much of it when the young people started, but I can see they've got something."

"It's changed so fast," put in Pepito Bonet, at sixty the youngest at the table. "Jaime Altet, who's about Paco's age, told me that when his father was dying six years ago, he urged Jaime to sell some of the land so as not to work as hard as he himself had all his life. But Jaime's glad now he didn't let any of it go."

"Times have changed," agreed the man who was seventy-three. "If my father could come back for just an hour or two to see how things are now, he wouldn't believe it. I wish he could, just to see."

The old men shook their heads, frowning in disbelief.

Five weeks after his father's death, Paco bought a tractor, a brave, bright-yellow one that roared past our house a dozen times a day, with Paco grinning boyishly at the wheel. "In one day, I can do what took me four before!" he exclaimed. "And without even getting tired! It's changed my whole life."

Grandmother Solé eyed the tractor with resentment. "It's as though he'd forgotten," she said, watching Paco's delight through her tears, "and so soon!"

It was not that Paco did not understand. Once he said to me he used to think it hardest to be widowed young, but he now saw it was still harder when you're old, after such a long life together.

One day six months later, without a word to anyone, Grandmother Solé had a television installed. When Paco came home from the fields, he saw the aerial on top of the house and found her, black skirts flaring in a bell around the stiff wooden chair, face a foot from the screen, watching a wrestling match. She said nothing more about the tractor, and Paco made no comment on the television. Nevertheless, it took all of us by surprise when she decided to join us on an outing. With her husband not yet buried a full year, doing anything pleasurable was a flagrant breach of tradition.

One evening a television program on marine life was just ending when Paco arrived from the fields for supper; I was chatting with Sara and Grandmother Solé. Although

Paco had little use for television, he watched the end of the program with interest.

"I've never been to the sea," he said. "I've seen it in Barcelona, in the port, but I've never been to a real beach."

"Where I grew up, we used to go once a year," Grandmother Solé said. "The village I grew up in was about fifteen kilometers away from it, but we only saw the sea on the feast of San Jaime, July 25th. Everyone went that day." A line of carts, each laden with baskets of food, quarts of wine, and the whole family—grandmother, grandfather, parents, children, all headed from the village for a day at the sea. Every cart was newly repainted, the mule, shiny from grooming, had new tassels and a straw hat for the sun, and there was a carpet for the family to sit on. She smiled, remembering. "No one went in the water, of course, but we spent the whole day on the shore." The women squealed in delighted fear at the edge of the waves, their huge skirts and petticoats growing heavier and heavier with seawater, while the men waded in with their trousers rolled up to pull the bolder children back to land. At noon they cooked a paella of salt cod and rice on the sand, took a siesta in the shade of the umbrella pines that came right down to the beach, and then headed home in a line of carts and mules for an evening of pastry, wine, and bonfires in the street.

"Why don't we all go?" I said. "It's not far by car."

Paco and Sara agreed eagerly. To our astonishment and perhaps her own as well, Grandmother Solé, who had not gone farther than Riera in ten years, seized the opportunity with alacrity. "I'd like to see it again," she said, "just to see how it's changed . . . It's good to see things," she added. "Now I wish I'd gone with you and José to Barcelona for San Juan. If I'd only known . . ."

As in all expeditions with our neighbors, we started out

very early in the morning in order to have a long, long day ahead, though it would take less than two hours to reach the shore of Calafell, the beach Grandmother Solé had known years ago. On the way, we were to stop in Riera to deliver to Josefina a sweater her grandmother had knitted. Josefina was living in one of the new, barrackslike apartment buildings that had begun to encircle the town, obliterating the old medieval silhouette with its cement rectangles. Because neither Grandmother Solé nor I had seen Josefina's apartment, we all had to go up.

The cement stairway was unpainted, the ceiling low and cold, lit brightly by bare neon tubes. Josefina proudly showed us the tiny apartment crammed with large pieces of furniture, all glossily varnished. The refrigerator—gleaming, white, proud, and expensive—stood next to a lowering commode. A heavy-legged dining table, a splay-footed cupboard with glass doors showing off a large collection of cheap cut glass, ten vinyl-covered chairs of monstrous proportions, and a baby buggy in which Josefina's two-month-old son slept soundly through the commotion—all made it nearly impossible to move through the front room, which was the usual combined dining and living room.

"I like modern things," Josefina kept repeating. "Everything I have is modern. I don't like things that are old and out-of-date!" Even the traditional picture of the Last Supper, a standard feature of every dining room in Las Casas, had been banished in favor of a calendar with a large photograph of a waterfall, a sight everyone in this dry land dreamed of seeing one day.

The kitchen, with its ceramic sink and running water (cold only), was much admired, and we were treated to a full display of household linens, enough to furnish a small hotel, stacked tightly and neatly in two ceiling-high wardrobes that took up all the space left in the bedroom by the double bed. Josefina waved us out, her newly acquired bulk almost filling the doorway. From now on, she would get fatter and fatter like other wives of rising young artisans and masons in Riera, who spent their time polishing their tiny apartments, coveting possessions to fill them, gossiping and eating chocolates on hot afternoons behind closed shutters.

All along the road from Riera, there were exclamations at the changes that had taken place. Many of the fields we passed were untilled and untended, the grapestalks bare, the olive and almond trees shriveling, the terraces built centuries ago serving only to record the obstinacy of the men who made them. From time to time, the road passed a solitary farmhouse. High-walled like citadels against marauders and bandits, most of them were empty, their two-foot-thick mud and stone walls beginning to sag and crack in neglect. No one wanted to live in such isolation anymore, and it was not worth it for the little profit to be had tilling rocky little mountain fields where no cart could fit, much less a tractor, and there was no way of tilling except by walking behind a mule and a bicycle-thin plow. *Es así*, the peasant living here said a generation ago, accepting a lifetime of hardship and solitude because he could not imagine anything else.

Even if there were peasants willing to remain, the interior would be abandoned perforce. Land that cannot be farmed by modern methods, like the terraced hill strips here and around Las Casas, is condemned. Villages like Las Casas are doomed, no matter what the villagers try. José Solé had tried in his way. His son was trying, trying new methods, new machinery, new investments, new produce, a new approach. It was of no use. The days were numbered for the small, independent farmer. He was an anachronism, belonging to a past that was dying and beyond recall, and his disappearance was only a matter of time.

On a side road not far from Riera, we saw a picturesque

silhouette on a hill, the ruins of a castle, a church, and a cluster of houses within an old wall. "Looks abandoned," Paco remarked. "You could probably buy a whole village like that for almost nothing." We decided to go see it.

It is an eerie feeling to walk into a recently deserted village. Signs of abandonment surrounded it. The olive and almond trees encircling the walls were scraggly, unpruned, and unproductive; the dry stony ground was overgrown with weeds and field grass. As we started down one of the streets, a chameleon scurried out of a cracked wall, startling us. Then a gaunt hound wriggled forward in cautious delight; another, less trusting, howled a warning; two old people unexpectedly appeared, one half blind, the other lame.

"There's nobody left," they told us.

"But you're staying on?" Paco asked.

They made a gesture of resignation. Perhaps they had nowhere to go. Perhaps they were too old to change. Who knows?

"There weren't nearly so many abandoned fields and empty houses when I came this way ten years ago," Paco remarked as we drove on. "Almost all the farms were worked. Well, I can see why they'd leave a place like this if they had somewhere else to go. But in Las Casas it's different. The land's better, the valley fields are flat and easy to work. Yet, the baker is talking of leaving now, and his next-door neighbor has just gone to a factory. Six or seven men from Las Casas are leaving the land every year now, and there aren't many of us left. It's a new thing." He shook his head slowly, adding that the former owners of our house, who moved to Barcelona the year we came, nine years ago, had been among the first to leave.

"Farming is a hard life," I said.

"It's a hard life," Paco agreed, "but if you add it all up, it doesn't come to eight hours a day, counting winter and the rains and all. I don't see how they can give it up and go to work for someone else. A peasant is his own boss. Why, if I want to go mushroom hunting one day or on an outing like this, there's no one to tell me no. Maybe I'll decide not to because I want to get something done, but it's my own decision. Give that up to take orders?" He shook his head vigorously. "And once you leave, there's no going back. It's gone. You sell your mule and cart, but that's the least of it. Once a vineyard is abandoned, it takes too much to get it to produce again. Look at that field."

We looked at the field of black stumps with a few puny, infested, yellowed leaves twittering from the scraggly ends of brittle branches. Abandoned only two summers, the field would have to be entirely replanted, Paco told us, and that meant plowing under the old vines and leaving the land for other crops for four or five years. Grafted and cared for, the new vines would start to bear in about three years more, but it would be longer before they yielded a full crop. "No, if the baker leaves—and it looks like he plans to—he's stuck in the new job whether he likes it or not," Paco said.

"What's he going to do?" I asked.

"Work for a baker in Riera. It's a full-time job, not like here, where he only bakes once every three days or so, now so many people have left. Everything's mechanized in the town bakery. No more loading the oven with brushwood and clearing it out, or mixing the dough by hand. But he may be sorry later. Though, what with selling less bread and having bad land that's not even his own, and the rent on it raised, he's probably been having a hard time making ends meet. Even the rich are finding land doesn't pay anymore. The Miros want to sell their land, but who would buy, and at the price they're asking?"

"Carlos gets social security in the new job," Sara added. "That counts too. And he'll get his salary as baker week in

156

and week out, while if we can't work or there's a bad harvest, we don't earn anything. I can see why he's leaving. I think Rosetta's happy about it."

I nodded, thinking of the many times I had seen the landowners Carlos rented from helping themselves to his vegetable patch, filling sacks and baskets, though Carlos paid in rent, not shares, for the use of the land. "If they would at least ask . . ." was his strongest complaint. When I became indignant on his behalf, he said, "What can I say to them? They should know better, but I can't say anything for a few tomatoes, I'd be ashamed to."

"Funny to think of the bakery empty," said Grandmother Solé. "We've always had a baker."

"Maybe things will get better," Paco said, frowning. "They have to. Why, 54,000 pesetas [about $770] is all I earned last year on wine. It's not worth growing it for that. I waited and waited, hoping the price would go up, but it didn't. And look at the baker. He built a shed for hens to try to earn extra money, and just when they started to lay, he was forced to sell them all to pay for the feed they'd eaten. That doesn't make sense."

I had thought the government regulated agricultural prices.

"It does," Paco explained, "but feed and sprays stay high and what we sell is kept low. I just don't get it. And then, we have to use more and more sprays to keep going. Nobody ever heard of mildew in my father's day, or hardly any of the diseases we have now. Plants that never had anything before are coming down with some new plague every year."

"It's sad," said Grandmother Solé, staring out the window. "All those houses and walls there for hundreds of years standing empty now, and olive and carob trees planted by someone's great grandfather running wild. When you think how the family must have waited for the trees to

157

have fruit! Maybe you think vineyards are slow growing," she said, turning to me, "olives are much slower."

"We have a saying, you know," Paco put in, smiling, "that he who plants an olive will never pick its fruit. He'll never live long enough."

As we came nearer the sea, we saw more and more cars on the road, and carts became infrequent. Many of the cars were foreign, but the majority belonged to the growing new class of Spanish consumers—workers and shopkeepers whose earnings have been rising continuously for the past five or six years, and who are eagerly aspiring to a grander style of living on credit. Hordes leave Barcelona every Saturday in their newly bought, installment-plan cars. Paco told us that a friend who has a gas station remarked that the tanks of many of these cars were never filled with more than the two or three gallons of gas needed to get the car wherever it was headed and back home, where it would sit on the street till its owner could afford another few gallons the following payday to set it in motion again. There are so many new cars on the road that it can take three or four hours to cover fifty miles in the radius of Barcelona on a Sunday or Saturday night, particularly along the sea.

I kept thinking how recent all these changes were. It was just after we moved to Las Casas that the tourist wave swept down the beaches of the eastern Mediterranean coast, littering them with tall, glassy apartment buildings, bungalows, snack bars, cheap hotels, restaurants, campsites, and nightclubs, turning the coast into one long sinuous honky-tonk boomtown stretching almost without interruption from the French border south. Already the seacoast was almost glutted, and speculators were reaching inland. Housing developments were more common than gas stations. There was even one just ten miles beyond Riera, a tract of paved streets, empty lots, lampposts that had rusted without ever bearing a light bulb, abandoned vineyards, and a model house with publicity banners advertising the future glories of the site. Sara laughed when we passed it. Inside, she said, there was a sales representative who would turn a faucet on full in the model kitchen to show prospective buyers the abundance of water, but the water was brought in by truck to a hidden container to fool the public.

"Sometimes the buyer doesn't care," Paco said, "because it's all speculation anyway. He only buys to wait for prices to go up in order to sell again. There's few that actually build on lots like this or believe the publicity." He paused a moment, then chuckled and told us of a man he knew in Riera who, as part owner of the development, became so taken by the spell he was weaving for buyers, that he ended up believing what he himself knew to be lies.

Near the coast, where vineyards and olive groves once led a patterned dance to the sea, a razed land is cross-hatched with roads, pockmarked with metal lampposts, and, as the sea becomes visible, covered more and more densely with little modern houses and towering apartment buildings.

"This was just a little fishing village with fishermen living on the beach and farmers living inland," Grandmother Solé remarked, regarding with awe the seven- and eight-story hotels of Calafell, taller than any buildings she had seen in her life. "How beautiful!" she and Sara cried.

As we drove into town, they exclaimed over the glass and neon fronts of apartment houses, condominiums, and hotels; they stared at bars with their signs in five languages advertising flamenco and guitar, both essential to the tourist image of Spain, though out of character in Catalonia. They could not understand my lack of enthusiasm for the new buildings or my delight in finding a stretch of four or five old blocks of fishermen's houses, tiny, two-storied, flat-roofed, and square, in faded pink, blue, and yellow, their front doors opening directly on the sand. The fishermen's boats were lined up on the beach, broad, cumbersome boats, beached high, prows looming fifteen feet in the air, rounded sterns settled solidly in the sand.

We stopped in a small cheap restaurant in sight of the boats for wine and fresh fried sardines. "If you haven't seen the fleet go out, you must," said the old fisherman who ran the place single-handed.

It was hard to imagine how the boats would ever reach the water, but fishermen up and down the coast, undeterred by lack of ports, have been launching them nightly for a thousand years or more.

"You won't be seeing it much longer," the old fisherman said. "Used to be forty or fifty boats went out from here, now there's about twenty. My own boat's over there, rotting on the sand. My son wouldn't be a fisherman; he wants to be out with his girl at night, not bobbing around on the sea. I don't blame him—it's a hard life."

The men earn more now. As soon as crowds of tourists came to the seashore demanding fish, everybody else wanted to eat fish too, and what used to be cat food became a luxury. In the old days, fishermen went out winter and summer, every night that there wasn't a storm, but still earned so little they had to go to France to pick grapes at harvest time. "There's more of a living to be made now, but nobody wants to be a fisherman. It's too hard," the old man said.

"You were your own boss, at least," said Paco.

"Sure, I was my own boss. That meant if there was no fish, there was no food, though I worked as hard if I caught fish or not. If you stay to see the boats go out, come back, and I'll give you a real fishermen's dinner." We decided to stay.

The drama started at dusk. Next to each boat, three or

four men squatted around a fire, the economical Catalan fire of three or four thick straight branches pointing like the spokes of a wheel toward the lit center and pushed toward it as they burn. In the pot over each fire, the fishermen were cooking their supper—fish, rice, and garlic, quantities of garlic. After dinner the fires were put to another purpose, the melting of soap. As the black pots of soap were set over the fires next to each boat, the sunlight turned rosy and faded, leaving the hulks of boats and huddles of waiting men lit only by the flames, the moon, and the phosphorescent waves.

The hour of launching is determined by the tide and the state of the sea, the old fisherman told us, and up and down the coast the fleets set out from every fishing village at the same hour. But only two or three boats can be launched at a time because several crews are needed to get each boat into the water. The men gather in the moonlight around the three boats to be launched first; they began lifting the huge wood beams stacked nearby and placing them horizontally like railroad ties in a path leading from the stern toward the sea. You can hear the weight of the beams as they thud into position on the sand.

After brushing the beams with boiling soap, the men lined up to the left and right of each of the first three boats, braced their feet in the sand, and pushed with their backs and shoulders against the sides. With the chant, "*Aarii! Arrriii!* marking the rhythmic surges and pauses of the sweating men, the huge boat slides over the slippery beams, slow to move forward but all too quick to slip sideways. Only the unrelenting efforts of some twenty men, directed by one standing on the deck, hold it to its course. As it reaches the downward pitch of the shore's edge, the boat slips over the soaped beams with ever-increasing speed. At a quickening pace, a half-dozen men at a time repeatedly leave the sides of the boat to fetch more beams, soap them, and haul them in front of the stern. Everything is done rapidly to maintain the boat's forward motion and save the men's strength.

As the boat enters the water, stern first, tension mounts. Waves tossing the hull right and left make it difficult to keep the beams in place. Waist-deep in water, the men struggle to keep their footing while holding the bobbing beams down. The heaving stern threatens. The beams themselves become deadly weapons. Shouts are exchanged, faces are taut in the light from the boat's reflector lamps, until at last the boat is free of the sand and can be guided to deep water.

Three boats were in the water inside a quarter hour, but it took another hour or more before the men finished launching the fleet, all the big ones, and for each of those, two smaller boats with inverted floodlights that flank the larger vessels to entice sardines, mackerel, and tuna to the surface. Once launched, the fleet moved out in a neat row parallel to shore. A slow chug of motors replaced the shouts and grunts, the slap of beams tossed before the stern, and the pounding of the boats in the waves.

From the restaurant, where we ate a hearty meal of noodles cooked in oil and fish bouillon, followed by fish stew, we could see the line of lights across the horizon. They were still there when we headed home at midnight, and would remain there until dawn, when the fleet came in to sell its catch. As we climbed the foothills, we looked back to see them strung across the sea like a row of tiny diamonds, far beyond the garish new hotels, motels, and snack bars.

11 ❧

Outsiders

THE SEA is Catalonia's source of wealth today as it has always been, but it is no longer the fishermen who bring in riches, any more than it is the barrels of wine that once were rolled over these beaches and floated out to ships bound for South America, or Catalans setting out over the waves to conquer foreign lands and build an empire reaching to Greece. Nevertheless, it is the sea that is enriching Catalonia once again. All these apartments, hotels, motels, roads, cars, and crowds are there because the sea is there; the sea has drawn these hordes of people, who bring an economic explosion in their wake. How strange to realize that the sea, which once made Catalonia a great nation and is bringing it prosperity now, may destroy it as a cultural entity.

In the past, the Mediterranean carried Catalonia's influence abroad through conquests and trade. Now the sea attracts so many outside influences and so many outsiders, that the cultural as well as physical pattern of the entire region is being transformed. The greatest threat is posed by the thousands upon thousands of laborers from the south who settle permanently among the local population each year. For centuries, despite pressures and proscriptions from Madrid, Catalans have clung to their national heritage, their language, and traditions. The danger the newcomers pose is not so much economic competition, it is cultural suffocation, by sheer numbers. Catalans fear it.

"Found myself talking Spanish to my mule the other day," Paco remarked once, shaking his head. "There's so many southerners moving in, it's getting so when you meet somebody in Riera, or even here in Las Casas, you don't know what to speak, Spanish or Catalan, and you're safer starting in Spanish."

"I don't see why they won't learn our language, if they're going to live here," Sara said, pursing her lips. "*We* had to learn theirs in school because Catalan wasn't allowed."

"Perhaps it's hard for them to learn a new language," I said. "You've all spoken two tongues since childhood, but to them it's a new idea."

"It's not that it's difficult, it's lack of good will," Sara replied. "They don't even try, the grown-ups. The children learn right away, but the older people don't make any effort."

"The village has changed so, we hardly know it any more," the baker's wife said one day. "About half the people here are from outside, and soon they'll take over."

"We let them come to the café so long as they behave," Señor Pedro remarked, "but they aren't allowed to join— if they did, they'd have a voice in how it was run and it wouldn't be ours any more."

"We're as much outsiders as the southerners, if not more," I said, "yet you let my husband join the café."

"It may not be fair," Pedro answered, "but there are so many of them. Would it be fair to all of us who built the café and planned it to have it changed by newcomers? This way, if they don't behave, we can keep them out, like Manuel's brother. Let him get drunk and get into fights in Riera if he wants to, but not here. This is ours."

When we first moved to the village, almost everyone there was related. But by the time we had lived in the house five or six years, there was a village within the village, a group apart, living alongside in houses that gradually fell empty as their Catalan owners left the land and moved to Barcelona or Riera to work as taxi drivers and factory hands. The outsiders in our village all came from the same town, Villaverde, in the western province of Extremadura, bordering Portugal.

The name Extremadura is popularly believed to come from the Latin *terra extrema et dura*. As early as the sixteenth century, the harsh land drove its people abroad to seek their fortunes. It was the Extremeñans who conquered Peru and Mexico under their countrymen Cortés and Pizarro, who discovered the Pacific Ocean under another Extremeñan adventurer, Balboa. They are an extraordinary-looking people, the women stolid, granite-faced, like Soviet statues, the men lithe and lean. One can imagine the stone figures of the women watching, four and a half centuries ago, as their men rode off to conquer a new world. Now they seek their fortunes instead in Germany, France, and, most of all, the area around Barcelona.

The first three men left Villaverde together in 1957 to look for work near Barcelona. Eventually they settled in Riera, where there were jobs for all comers in the expanding brick and canning factories. When all Riera's available housing was occupied at rising rents, the newcomers spread to outlying villages like Las Casas. The families of the first three men joined them, and their relatives and neighbors followed until there were only a handful of old people and a few rich families left back home. Almost the entire town of Villaverde, mayor and priest included, moved five hundred and fifty miles northeast to settle around Riera.

Villaverde's case is not unique. It is only a small part of a mass movement in which thousands abandon the rural south of Spain every year for the industrialized north, the Basque coast, Madrid, and Catalonia. Attracted to the new jobs opened up by tourism and the economic expansion it engendered, the migrations are part of the social and economic upheaval that is changing the face of Spain. Where the first migrants settle and find jobs, the rest of the town will follow, forming ever-growing enclaves in which they re-establish their old lives as best they can, live according to their native customs, associate mainly with relatives and neighbors from back home, and keep alive a fierce love for their own land and for their native town.

I had gradually come to understand Extremeñans through our housekeeper, who lived with her husband, Manuel, and six children four doors up the street. Amalia worked sullenly at first, then more cheerfully as she came to regard me as a fellow foreigner. Like the other Extremeñans, she always spoke of her province with love, longing, and pride, beginning sentence after sentence in the singsong voice of her countrymen, "In my land, *en mi tierra*, we have—" and everything she named was bigger and better and more abundant or more beautiful than anywhere else, especially here in Las Casas. Manuel told of partridge and grouse so plentiful the land is one of Franco's favorite hunting grounds. Manuel's father spoke of mushrooms growing wild everywhere, of enormous turtles one could catch and eat for days so that no one had to go hungry, ever.

"And the water, there's so much of it, and such soft water! It made you feel good just to walk past the fountains!" said Amalia. "There were always flowers in the windows. People took pleasure in things. Even in the capital of a province, you wouldn't find a church such as we had, a mosque the Moors built, but now it's a church with statues in the richest clothes you've ever seen, all covered with precious jewels, silks, and satins, that people come from far away to see. You could sit in your own doorway and watch the world go by. Here," she pouted in contempt, "there's nothing. In winter there isn't even anybody in the street. At first I thought I couldn't live here, it made me so sad. Nothing happens, nothing goes by. All you can see is the highway, a way off, and a few cars on it from time to time."

The villagers, equally proud of Catalonia, its language and artistic heritage, sometimes lose patience. "Why didn't you stay there if it was so good?" they say. The answer is always the same: "There's no living there."

"I couldn't go back to living that way again," Amalia said, "all the men lining up in the town square every day and the overseers saying, 'You, you, and you work.'" The rest would just have to go home empty-handed. Good men, too, sometimes. Strong and willing. There were times when nobody had any work at all, depending on the season.

"All the land belonged to just four families, and all they thought of was themselves. Parts of the year there was no work at all, and then there was no money either. It was good land too—rich land, not like around here," she smacked her lips in contempt. "There were fields of olives that grow big, plump, and juicy, not like the hard little ones here that have no meat on them, grapes that made some of the best wine you ever tasted, rich and strong, and fields of wheat as far as you could see. One landowner had a hundred men working for him all year, and sometimes there were ninety of us women, flaying fava beans, scything wheat. We used to go out early enough in summer to get to his fields at four in the morning, five or six miles away.

It was hot, so hot when you finished at twelve and had to walk back in the sun that by the time you got home, you didn't want to do anything, not even eat, just go to bed. Hardly any women go to the fields anymore, but I went a lot until I was married."

"What do the rich do, the ones that stayed, now the men have left?" I asked.

"They still have some families that live on the place and have worked for them forever. Those don't leave. One rich man has land covering four provinces, with houses for the workers and a school for their children. But for most things they use machinery now. Instead of hiring men, they buy machines."

"There must be a lot of land abandoned."

"There is, I hear. I haven't been back," she said. "I'd like to, to visit, if I could save up enough money, but I never can. Something always happens."

I nodded. The villagers had told me her husband gambled his small, irregular salary away one week out of two.

"My aunt went back last Christmas and said it was sad to see. In her street, which is one of the main streets of the town, there are only four or five houses still open. In the next street, that leads to the palace the Moors built, there are six or seven; in the next, two or three, and a few more in the center of town along with a shop or two, but the rest of the town is abandoned. And what a beautiful town it is . . . makes you sad to think . . . white everywhere and full of flowers. There's no taste here, no pride."

The contempt is mutual.

"They come as peons and stay peons," said Paco. "Never learn anything, never save anything. If a Catalan had the bad luck to have to go get a job like that, if he didn't have any land and had to work for somebody else, he'd become a foreman in time or a mason's assistant, if not a mason. He'd work his way up. But these people are always going to be peons."

"Joselito made good," I reminded him. Joselito was the head of the first family from Extremadura to come to Las Casas, years in advance of the rest. He was now a mason with a number of men under him.

"He's the only one I know of," Paco answered. "Now *there* was a good family, hard-working people. We were all sorry when they moved to Riera. When they came from the south, they had nothing. They rented that hovel of a house with one broken chair in it for furniture and a pot or two for cooking in the fireplace, and now they have a car, a television, a refrigerator, and they've almost paid for their own house. But how that whole family worked! Four sons and the father and daughter and mother, all of them, seven days a week. And they saved. Yes, they were serious."

Sara laughed. "They're serious now, but remember how happy-go-lucky they were when they first came, poor as they were? Makes you wonder. One of their neighbors, Pepe, told me a funny story about Joselito. When he first came and they were so poor, he used to set out on foot to get to his job as peon very early. It was long before light in winter, but he always left the house singing. Every morning Pepe would hear him leave singing. One day Joselito bought himself a bicycle. He could leave a bit later on the bike. Pepe knew he did because he always heard him singing as he went." Sara paused. "Then Joselito got a motorcycle. After that, he used to leave much, much later, but always in a great hurry, and from that day on, he never sang as he left."

I remember old José Solé and Alfonso Miret telling me of the singing in the café in the old days. I thought of Amalia singing Arabic melodies while she scrubbed or whitewashed our house. I wondered aloud if prosperity brought sadness.

"I don't know," they said. "Maybe as soon as you have something, you're afraid of losing it, and you lose your freedom instead. Still, you can't say it's better to be poor."

All the immigrants from Villaverde were poor. All lived hard lives, though better ones than they had known before. When Amalia arrived in 1961, one of the first Extremeñans to settle in the village, she had been separated from her husband for four years while he went from place to place, looking for an area where jobs were plentiful and he could house his large family: six children, his wife, himself, and his father. He had worked for six months asphalting a new highway but was let off when the job was completed; he had worked for four months completing a hotel on the coast but was out of work again when the job was done. Because it was easy for contractors to find unskilled labor whenever they needed it, they dropped men as soon as the job at hand was finished. In Riera, Manuel heard, there seemed to be a more constant demand for workers in the new factories and the building of new housing for the consequent expansion of the town, all of it a result, directly or indirectly, of the tourist boom on the coast. In Riera, rents were too high for the space he needed, but Manuel found a house in Las Casas that was cheap and roomy. It was also barely habitable. There was no well, no water, no indoor plumbing. The roof leaked, the walls sagged, and the chimney smoked so heavily it was not possible to build a fire. Amalia cooked on a tiny oil burner, lit a charcoal brazier for the family to sit around on cold winter nights, caked layers of whitewash over the cracked walls inside, and whitewashed the outside of the house around the doors and windows as far as an arm could reach. She quarreled constantly with the landlord over the caving floor and broken windowpanes while the children barely escaped injury when the floor gave way, and the winter wind whistled through the broken glass.

"Why not patch up the windows yourselves if the landlord won't?" I asked.

"There are too many windows," Amalia said. "If it were

just one, but there isn't a window that will close. He charges enough, he should do it."

"There's no profit in it," the landlord claimed. "These people pay a pittance because the house is old, and then they expect me to make it like new for the same miserable money. It wouldn't pay."

Manuel and Amalia stayed because there was nowhere they could go. All the houses were filled, and the expensive, new little apartments in Riera were too small for a family of nine.

"Six children! They never think about the future," the Catalans said in contempt. "They have all those children and buy them more shoes and toys than they can afford, all on time—why, there are families here that owe for Christmas toys bought three years back. They've probably paid for them twice in interest, but they never think of that. Never think of anything."

"These Catalans don't have children because the men are cold, frigid!" said Amalia with contempt. Homely as a mudhole, she had borne six sons to her handsome husband and was proud of it.

"They shouldn't have children if they can't take care of them," the villagers said. "They just let them run wild. And in school, where there are more outsiders than ourselves now, the teacher can't teach anymore because she has to spend all her time keeping order."

"My son's always being sent home," Manuel said. "How can he learn if the teacher sends him out of school?"

"I want him to go somewhere where he'll learn so he can get into a trade. I don't want him to go to the fields," said Amalia. "If he has to, then he has to, but it's no life. When I asked my next-door neighbor if my son might have a chance to get into a government trade school, she wouldn't even tell me how to go about it. Why shouldn't he have a chance? Aren't we all equal before God? Just because there was no work where we lived doesn't mean we're worse than they."

When Amalia and her husband bought a television set —on time, of course—Amalia resented her neighbors' remarks. "They're not paying for it, why should they care?" she said.

"Ah, they just don't know how to live," Manuel said. "Look how their houses are all dark after sunset because they're inside with the shutters pulled counting their money. Bah! Misers! You go to a bar in my country, everybody drinks together and talks. I buy him one, he buys me one, no one keeps track. Here, if a Catalan goes to a bar, he goes alone, or if he's with another fellow, they divide up the bill like drawing up a contract."

The Extremeñans in the village never had any money put aside. With four, five, six, or more children per family, clothes and shoes alone kept the family on the edge of poverty, even if the father brought home his entire weekly salary of 1,500 pesetas (roughly twenty dollars). Often he didn't bring it home. If he didn't gamble like Manuel, he would go from bar to bar on payday like Manuel's brother, buying wine or cognac for all until there were only a few hundred pesetas left. To drink was to be *hombre*. Let the women worry about feeding the children suppers of tomatoes and rice, or tomatoes and bread, or stretching a pound of fish around a table of nine. And let them wait without protest until the man of the house is good and ready to come home with whatever is left.

Amalia's daily life was a tragicomic series of disasters, partly self-induced, partly inflicted by a puckish fate. The cloth Amalia bought so cheaply from a traveling vendor in the open market on Friday fell apart when she started to sew it, and there was no way to take it back. The light fixture over the dining table that everyone had noticed was loose fell, at last, into the Sunday stew with a spatter of broken glass just as Amalia was about to ladle out dinner. A cat that walked in the open street door was caught finishing the last of the pound of sardines constituting Monday's supper. Amalia's ten rabbits died of galloping diarrhea within a week of growing large enough to be eaten. The dog polished off the only rooster, and the hens died soon afterward of either melancholy or disease. The youngest child put a week's salary into the burning brazier, and no one realized those were peseta notes, not bits of newspaper, until they were too burned to return to the bank. The secondhand bicycle Manuel bought to get to work proved unusable and unrepairable within a week. His father fell off a ladder and broke his hip just when Manuel had changed jobs and had not re-established his social-security insurance. A month later, another child was on the way, Manuel was out of a job again, and the store was threatening to reclaim the television set.

There were few outings for Amalia. Like other Extremeñan men, Manuel sought his amusement without her, returning from work after stopping off in bars for food and wine, going out alone on Saturday nights and Sundays. The only annual family excursion was to the town fair in Riera. Each year, Amalia swore she would never go again because her children demanded rides on every merry-go-round and auto-shock rink, wanted to buy every bit of tinsel or candy sold, wailed at not having their way, got lost, got sick, fell in puddles, tore their Sunday clothes. Desperate, Amalia would threaten never to take them anywhere again, and they, thinking this outing was the last in all their lives, would become wilder and more demanding than ever.

Once Amalia was invited to go by train to a wedding in a town fifty miles distant, the marriage of one of numerous relatives who had settled in the Barcelona region. I looked forward to the excursion for her, admired the dress she had made, the clothes she had managed to put together for the children. When she came to the house the following day, I was eager for details of what I assumed had been a rare treat. "Never again," she said. "From now on, I'll stay home and be thankful for it. The train was so crowded only three of us could sit at a time. It was so hot no one could breathe, but there was nothing to drink. The train broke down at least four times on the way, once in a station where they were selling cold drinks at a buffet right in front of us, but we didn't dare get off because we didn't know how long it would be. As it turned out, we stopped so long we were late for the wedding and had just time to greet everybody and turn around and take the next train right back because it was the last one, and we rode home with the children crying all the way because nobody had had a drink of water or a bite to eat since morning."

In 1968, when disorders in France and restrictions on money elsewhere kept Europeans at home, there was a crisis in Spain. Much of the economic expansion was on credit, on speculation, and on the assumption the tourists would keep coming. When they stopped, the bubble burst. Apartments and hotels were empty, construction was suspended, factories laid off workers, salaries were cut, thousands were without work or any prospect of getting it.

Amalia and her family and all the rest of the Extremeñans in Las Casas survived the crisis. There was always someone with a job among these large families with their numerous relatives, and the rest lived off him somehow.

Paco was not sorry for them, even in the hard times of 1968. "There's work for men who stayed with one boss," he said. "Those without jobs are the ones who switch when a new construction company comes to town and offers two cents an hour more, or maybe even ten or twenty if the job has to get done in a hurry. Thing is, once the job's done, there's no more work there. The men are stranded, and the boss they left in a period of full work isn't going to take them back in a lull, though he'll keep paying the ones who stayed with him." He shook his head. "It's too bad they had to leave their own country, but if they don't get on here, it's their own fault. A man's got to think ahead because there'll always be bad times as well as good ones."

For Amalia, whose husband gambled and was often jobless, for her sister-in-law, whose husband drank his earnings every Saturday, and for most of the outsiders I knew around Riera, there was no thinking ahead. Any plans or hopes were promptly waylaid by disaster, but at least they were not hungry. Perhaps that was enough.

12 &

The End

In 1969 the number of tourists in Spain reached a new peak. The crisis of 1968 was forgotten. Along the coast, the clang of construction and the rumble of trucks carrying building materials drowned out the sounds of the sea and the wind in the olives. Every hotel, rooming house, condominium, and villa was filled; campers' tents and buses were strung along the beaches in an almost solid line. In Riera, too, the building was frantic. The stone quarry, just outside town, had five times as many workers as it had had two years ago. There were four new factories employing more than two hundred men each, more than enough to replace the three outmoded tile factories with their wood-stoked kilns and handful of workers that had constituted Riera's main industry five years before. The townspeople were making more money than they had ever dreamed possible. Shopkeepers modernized their storefronts, changed old-fashioned, dim interiors clogged with barrels of olives and sardines into neat corridors of self-service, where the wooden box of coins was replaced by a ringing cash register. Masons drove through town in Mercedeses, inspecting the new apartment buildings spreading further and further beyond Riera to house the influx of workers from the south. Spanish was heard more often on the streets than the native Catalan. Housewives who used to buy chicken wings were topping their full market baskets with expensive shrimp and cray-fish and taking a few extra turns around the square so that all could admire their extravagance.

During the long warm season the town teemed with tourists stopping to buy or eat. Somber old women in black turned to stare at a hairy-chested German in pink plaid sport shirt or a middle-aged Frenchwoman in a gold lamé playsuit. When the first tourists arrived in Riera, peasants and townspeople were indignant about their dress. The tourists, they felt, had abandoned all decorum as if they were among savages. "They wouldn't go around like that in their own country, would they?" I was asked more than once. But soon the strangely dressed tourists were no longer exclusively foreign. Spaniards from the inland cities of Zaragoza and Huesca, miserly and strict until the recent boom, began pouring forth in slacks and gaudy holiday clothes to the beaches via Riera and other once tranquil towns. Traffic jams blocked the narrow streets, and horns blared as drivers sweated angrily in the hot sun.

Looking at the passing parade from the doorway of one of his favorite bars, the town carpenter shook his head. It was only fifteen years ago, he told me, that a car stopping in Riera was the object of intense interest and curiosity, and a foreigner was received with the hospitality of the days when travelers were a welcome and unique source of news of the outside world. A mere thirty years ago, when he was a young man, the town had been a world in itself, delimited by the almond and olive trees on its perimeter. Newspapers were four or five days old before they reached the town from Barcelona, though it was only thirty miles away; mails were erratic, the telephone (which hasn't improved much) was almost unusable, and cars, radios, and movies were practically unknown. Touring professional and local amateur theater companies played on Saturdays, Sundays, and holidays to large audiences, whose appreciation was no more diminished by the consumption of garlic sausages and wine during the performance than by the squealing of babies, sleepy by the time the evening performance started at 11:00 P.M.

The population then must have been no more than 4,000, but to hear the carpenter talk of it, at least 3,000 were eccentrics, pursuing their antisocial or extravagant bents with no thought of changing their ways. There was the ill-tempered shoemaker who would snatch a shoe from your hand and hurl it contemptuously into the street if he thought it beyond repair. There was the tailor who would ask a customer ordering a suit to take three turns around the public square in front of his shop and, after measuring the man with his eyes alone, produce the finished suit in a week. There was the iceman who wrote verse and knew where every delicacy could be gathered free: where the mussels were largest, the clams thickest; where the first mushrooms would spring up under the prickly mountain brush after the October rains, and where to dig in the fields for the wild asparagus that ripened in March. There were many passionate collectors—of anything from matchboxes and bottle caps (bottle caps at least were useful for making curtains to keep out the flies) to pieces of Stone Age silex and shards of Roman amphorae.

Only in winter, and only away from the center of Riera, do you still have a glimpse of the past, of the old, slow, bucolic rhythm that converts time into one unending day with no beginning or close. In the quiet town, people think and talk of life and death again instead of money and the outside world. With the tourists gone, the cafés again have only their habitués: the card players, the contemplative, resigned old men, the artisans and shopkeepers and bank directors who drop in and out for a glass of wine or a coffee laced with cognac or a bite to eat. On any given day, you will find the same people in the same café at the same hour and probably at the same table. The streets smell of manure and hay. The blacksmith still shoes horses in the middle of one of the main arteries; the carpenter strips an old desk of paint in the street; the baker piles up his pine boughs there. As in the village, the street is a community living room. The women sit, alone or in groups, embroidering and crocheting with their backs to the street. If you stop to talk, someone will offer you a chair. But these are only small corners of the town, pockets of the past, where newcomers from the south and from the surrounding villages have not poured in, and the old houses have not yet been torn down to make way for the apartment buildings more profitable to landlords and speculators.

Like other villages throughout the inland hills and mountains of Catalonia, Las Casas del Torrente was being gradually deserted. By 1970 there were more empty houses than occupied ones in Las Casas. More Catalans had left the land. Though some of them commuted to Riera's factories, others, like the baker, had moved to Riera to be near work, and many had gone to Barcelona. Extremeñans like Amalia and Manuel, their in-laws, brothers, and uncles, were moving out of Las Casas into new apartments in Riera. The house we had seen on our first visit to the village, rented for years by three Extremeñan families, stood empty again.

"It's more modern," Amalia explained when she announced her departure. "There's not as much room, but we can heat it in winter, the children can go to a decent school, and even if the rent is much higher, we'll make out better. My husband and the two older boys won't have to take the bus to work every day. Back and forth, three fares add up in a week, you'd be surprised how much. And I can buy in the market every day where it's cheaper."

All the peasants saw of the new prosperity was rising retail prices that narrowed the profit they made on their crops. More and more farmers like Paco were being driven off the land, but though it seemed to Paco that if the grapes and melons he and others like him grew did not reach the market in Riera, there would be a shortage of food, Spain's agricultural production was actually increasing every year as the small patchwork plots yielded to large-scale mechanized farms. There was no profit in Paco's farming. Not only was there no profit for him, there was no profit for Spain. The country could no longer afford to have a man spend his life cutting wayside weeds that grew back at once, like the wiry old man we watched during our first years in Las Casas, nor could it afford to have men devote a lifetime to tilling a handful of rocky patches.

In the summer of 1970, the Ministry of Agriculture sent experts to our region, and I assume to others, to make factual case studies of three kinds of farmers: large landholders, middle-size landholders, and small farmers. Those selected were asked to have on hand figures on production, expenditures, and income from each of their crops. One of the small farmers was a good friend of Paco's.

The government expert asked the farmer how many hectoliters of wine he produced, what he spent on sprays, fertilizer, and grape pickers, and what he sold the wine for. When he had all those figures written down, the expert paused. "But you can't live on that," he said. "You aren't making any money." It was the same for the man's other produce: his melons, his chickens, his pigs. Each time the expert repeated that it was impossible, that there was no livelihood in it. At last, the farmer answered back angrily, "But you know very well there's no living on it because

181

it's you who set the prices for the things I have to buy and the prices for what I sell. You should be the first to know I can't live on it!"

Making a small margin of profit on a large scale is a new idea not suited to this region of small plots and independent peasants. "I thought the large chicken farms stood to lose," Paco told me one day, "because we small farmers don't pay for labor, and don't count in money the hours we spend feeding, cleaning, watering, vaccinating. Paying for all that on top of the feed and serums and all, I figured you couldn't make money. It seems I was wrong. Instead, it's the small farmers that are going out of business, while the large chicken farms that have to hire workers are growing larger and more prosperous. They can afford to make only a tiny profit on each chicken because they have so many, and they have enough reserves that an epidemic in one coop doesn't put them out of business the way it has so many small farmers like me."

One morning, I found Paco leaning on the stone wall overlooking his nearest field. He turned to face me and said, "I'm leaving, too." I paused a long time before answering, as the villagers do when confronted with something startling or new. Years ago I would have answered glibly, filling in the silence while thinking. All I could think was that if Paco, the ideal poster peasant, was leaving, the village was finished.

"I'll be very sorry," I said at last. Then I shook my head, still half-disbelieving. "I never thought you would be one to leave."

"Neither did I," he answered. "If it hadn't come up as it did, perhaps I never would have left. I like being a peasant. I enjoy the work." He paused. "It wasn't always that way."

We both sat down on the wall. It was going to be a long talk. The early morning sun was hot, but the gnarled century-old carob tree at our backs spread a cool shade under its pendulant seedpods and broad leaves. Cuckoos called to each other across the red, oxidized earth, announcing a hot day. In front of us lay a field of olives, their leaves tilted upward as if the trees were extending a thousand cupped hands.

"Do you know when those trees were planted?" Paco asked. "My great-grandfather put them in, so that must have been over a hundred years ago. Some have died and been replaced since, but that's when the orchard was started." There was a silence.

"It's hard to leave it. There's a lot I'll regret, but . . ." a look of anger crossed his face, "they just don't let us make a living! I'm not afraid of hard work, I'm young still, and strong. I can do it, but if you can't put away a little for the bad years, there's no future in it." He looked as angry as I had ever seen him. Pausing to snap off a twig of rosemary growing next to the stone wall, he crushed it in his fingers. The smell of the sun-warmed herb tingled our nostrils. At our feet hundreds of scarlet, blue, and yellow field flowers managed to grow without water among the rocks and burned brown field grass.

"Farming can be a good life," Paco continued. "I didn't think so when I was a boy. When I was fourteen, I was sent to Barcelona to work in a bar owned by a distant relative—a great-uncle on my mother's side. I was delighted to go to the city, to get away from this little village and see lights, people, traffic! You know how the young are. Look at Carmen, she's having the time of her life. When I'd come back here for holidays, the village always looked sad to me, so quiet and empty, so dark after sunset. I couldn't imagine seeing the same faces every day. I didn't like working in the fields, getting dirty, and being a peasant, but my older brother, Antonio, had been killed in the war, so when my other brother, Pablo, was killed in an accident, I had to come back. I was twenty and how I hated it. I thought I'd never get used to the loneliness, the quiet. But now, I work with more pleasure every year. I look at my fields with satisfaction. I enjoy the peace and quiet, enjoy being my own boss. Maybe you work harder when you're your own boss, but it's worth it. Being a peasant is a good life, if you can just make a decent living. I'd have hung on a little longer, I suppose, if it hadn't happened the way it did."

Paco's cousin Pablo, Marina's father, had come out one recent Sunday with the son of the great-uncle who owned the bar Paco had worked in as a boy. Juan was the son's name, and he was looking for someone to help him run the bar, which had become suddenly popular and was expanding into a restaurant. "I told him I didn't know a thing about the restaurant business, but he claimed all he wanted was someone he could count on and who could learn. I went last week to look it over." Paco paused. "It looks like a good thing. Still, I wouldn't have agreed if it hadn't come up just when it did."

Then he told me the Miros had sold their land after all, and the new owner was taking everyone off.

I didn't understand.

"You see," Paco explained, "if a man works someone else's land on shares, he has first chance to buy if it's sold, but if he doesn't agree to the price and it's sold to someone else, he has to get off unless the new owner wants him to stay. He gets paid by the new owner for improvements —trees planted, or vines—but he loses the land. I could have bought, I suppose, but the Miros were asking too much—I never thought they'd sell it at that price. I could have looked for new land, too, but I'd had some of the best and wasn't making out. Then Juan came along just at the right moment, so—" he spread his hands in a Latin

184

gesture of yielding to fate, "this year will be my last harvest."

Sara, who had just come up the road with a bundle of greens for the goat on her head, heard Paco's last words. "Remember the first harvest?" she said to me, smiling. "The first one you helped us with and the way we celebrated it together? You had black hands like everyone else! Who was there that day?"

I remembered. "Carlos, the baker, and Rosetta, Tía María and Raimondo, the two of us, your parents, you two, and Pepe and Josefina, of course. Everyone has left but you and Pepe—and now you're leaving, too."

"Everything changes," Sara replied. "It's as God wills. At least Pepe will have a chance to get more education in Barcelona so when he grows up he can make a better living than a peasant."

"You want him to have clean hands," Paco teased her.

"I want him to make a living he can count on in good times and bad," Sara answered firmly. Changing the subject, she added, "Some people say they're going to set up a real vineyard on the Miro land with a manager and a bottling plant here and everything."

"It's some of the best land you could find for wine," Paco said, "but I don't believe that. Nobody makes money on wine anymore."

"But don't you know who bought it?" I asked.

"No, we only dealt with the Miros' agent. If anyone knows, no one is saying."

I would have felt more surprise had I not already learned that property ownership is often kept secret. When a house changed hands, the fact was usually concealed as long as possible; why, I never understood. Sometimes ownership remained secret forever. So far as I could tell, nobody except the man who managed it knew who owned the village's only olive press, and perhaps even he did not know; perhaps he dealt through an intermediary, as Paco and the other sharecroppers on the Miro land had.

"Maybe it's just speculation," Sara said. "Somebody buying in hopes it will rise in price like on the coast."

Paco shook his head. "At the price it was going for, I can't believe that either. It's too much money to invest unless you're sure what you're going to get out of it. The Miros owned a lot of land."

Together we traced the fields within our view that were —or had been—Miro property: all the rich fields sloping down on the far side of the village, most of the land this side of the *torrente,* and the gently rising slopes you pass for a mile or two when you approach the village from Riera, including all the almond trees that made a garland at the foot of the hilltop town in February when the pink and white blossoms burst forth.

I looked at it, feeling I was seeing it all for the last time, and the more I looked, the more I realized how much it had changed since that first day when we had drunk the good strong wine of the region. Deserted vineyards and orchards blighted the hills and valleys. Hastily erected (and often as hastily abandoned) chicken coops marred the once harmonious silhouette of red-tiled roofs. Tin-topped pigsties glittered at the edges of the village like a shantytown. The arched carriageways of half the houses had been squared off in the prosperity of the mid-sixties, and in many, metal garage doors had been installed for a newly acquired car or small truck.

As soon as any peasant earns a little money, he begins to fix up the house inside and out according to his newly acquired tastes and means. He tears out the old tile floors to replace them with linoleum, plasters rough cement over the whitewashed stone walls, and replaces the stone sink with shiny porcelain. Still, it has not escaped his notice that the old traditional things are favored by foreigners and rich people (terms roughly synonymous in Spain). Paco had teased me when he transformed the entrance to his house by fitting new, prefabricated cement steps over the old staircase with its worn tiles the color of the edges of a sunset, and its wood borders washed to the smooth gray of old dock boards. "You see, I'm leaving the old staircase underneath," he said, "just in case I strike it rich one day. Then I can simply rip off the new one and have an antique like the rich."

The changes in the village were not only physical. The café had had to close for lack of support, not just because there were far fewer villagers, but because those who stayed no longer counted on the café for entertainment. The old no longer filled a table, most of the middle-aged stayed home watching their own television sets, and the young preferred the nearest town for their fun. Even now, in summer, the streets were surprisingly empty. There were far fewer people, of course, but that wasn't all. I began to realize that despite adjoining walls, I sometimes didn't see my next-door neighbors for days. In the beginning, I had seen all the villagers constantly in the street, the women working, the men passing up and down in their carts and sitting on their doorsteps waiting for supper. Sometimes, after supper, the whole family would sit out in the street in the cool of the evening, chatting with each other and with neighbors. Now most of the men remaining worked outside the village, commuting to Riera or its outlying factories, and the women stayed in the house.

"I used to look forward to Monday," Sara said as if reading my thoughts. "It was a long walk to the village washing place with all the sheets and towels and clothes on your head, but it was a good way to spend the day, with twenty or thirty or more of us talking and laughing. Now we have running water, so we don't wash together. We have

187

motos and cars so we don't ride together and don't go the same places. Why, there are women still living here I don't see anymore that I always used to see on Mondays and at the baker's every day, twice a day. It still seems odd to see the bakery closed."

"Carlos says he's completely satisfied with his new life," I said.

"I don't believe it," Paco replied. "He may say so, but no man is ever satisfied."

"You know," Sara continued, "you hardly see anybody any more except in church, and fewer and fewer even there. There isn't the faith there used to be, or the respect. Why, I remember in the old days when the priest came through the village—on foot, mind you—to give the last rites to someone dying, women dropped to their knees in awe as he went by in his high collar with his heavy robes, ringing a bell at his side and carrying the big box with the Host and all the rest. When a relative died, the whole family gathered in the bedroom, kneeling and praying. I can remember kneeling, my sister, my mother and me all covered with heavy mantillas, when I was just a child. Nowadays," she gave a contemptuous chuckle, "the priest drives up to the door in his car like anybody else, jumps out, does his business, maybe without all the family even being present, and drives off."

"It was a good thing, though, to make the church democratic and treat everybody the same," Paco interjected. "Did you hear about the scandal when the mayor of Riera insisted his daughter should have a carpet in the church for her wedding and the priest refused? That was something new."

"What I remember is Tía María carrying that chair to Riera on foot," I put in.

It had been the custom for each family in the village to have a certain number of chairs, placed, by tradition, in

188

a particular spot in the church—a humble version of the family pew. When the order was promulgated that all seats within the church were to be alike and belong to no one, the chairs were reclaimed by the families owning them, and benches were substituted. Tía María's chair actually belonged to her son in Riera, and I had come across her carrying it down the hot highway one August day when I was driving to market. I had come along too late to help her much with my offer of a ride because she had already covered four of the six miles. But when I remarked that she must be exhausted from carrying the chair so far in such heat, she smiled. "Not at all," she said. "Every time I get tired, I just put the chair down on the road and sit in it a while."

"She was a great one, poor woman," Sara said. "She and her brother, the mason, were cut from the same cloth. But I'm afraid María's not for long now. She can't leave the house any more, even to go to church. Last time I saw her, she said she'd stopped taking confession because the new young priest who came to confess her told her a joke about some woman of eighty-five going to the beach in a bikini and now she won't have him in the house."

"Ah, that one," Paco smiled. "I hear after a good Sunday he'll swing proudly into Rosa Bonet's store next to the church and give his order with a grin. 'Meat today, Rosa. Collection went fine this morning, we'll have the best meat for dinner.'"

Sara sighed. "No wonder there's no respect. Thirty years ago, the priest used to walk here every day at noon in cold and heat and rain to teach the young people to sing the responses to mass. Today people stay ignorant and the priest gets in his car and drives off somewhere in the mountains or to the beach instead. Why, they don't even wear robes! Everything's changed."

"I was just thinking the other day of Josefina's wedding,"

said Paco. "That wasn't so long ago, but you probably couldn't do it today. First of all, half the people are scattered all over, and they wouldn't be free anyway. You can't just leave a job the way you can leave the fields if something you want to do comes up. We're all isolated now, each man in his house with his ambitions and himself."

You didn't see that twenty years ago, Paco and Sara agreed. Everybody used to thresh at the same time, harvest at the same time, pick olives together, and celebrate the end of every harvest together the way we had that first year. Everybody helped his neighbor. If a woman's husband fell sick, the other men in the village took turns doing his work. Now they might not even hear about it right away. There'd be a few words of sympathy maybe, or perhaps a close friend or relative would help out a bit . . . if he wasn't too busy.

"I barely saw Las Casas, then, as a real village," I said.

"You came in at the end," Paco agreed, "but you saw some of the best times because there was lots of misery in the old days. It was just when you came that we began really enjoying a full harvest. Things looked good. We thought they could only get better, but it didn't even last. And now," he spread his hands again in acceptance of fate, "Las Casas is going the way of that village we visited on the way to the sea last spring."

Paco moved out right after the grape harvest that fall of 1970. There were few villagers left for the dreary, cold task of picking olives bare-handed, shivering in the December wind to fill enormous sacks with the tiny fruit. Hands turn blue with cold and swollen with chilblains. The *tramontana* that crosses the snows of the Pyrenees is a piercing wind, howling and icy in clear sunny weather. The sea wind brings clammy gray days. The landscape is drab: black bare stalks of vines on the red-brown fields, denuded almond trees. Only the carob, the olive, and the pine are evergreen. Mud is deep in the streets. This Mediterranean land looks all wrong in wet and cold, and the only reassurance on a damp dark day lies in the bright green fields of wheat crisscrossing the land like a ribbon of hope.

I thought back to the year before, when on one of those damp dark days I joined Paco and his wife to test the new olive oil. Warmed by a wood furnace, that heats the oil for pressing, and filled with the rich aroma of hot, freshly made oil, the olive press is the nicest place to be in winter. There were always several men working, usually several others kibitzing, and toward evening a few men and women gathered to try the oil. Like them, we brought huge loaves of bread, toasted slices on long forks over the open flames of the stove, and then dipped the bread into the hot, golden oil as it poured from the press and refining machinery into the last, huge tiled vat sunk in the floor. I remembered the feeling of biting into the crusty, warm bread, so swollen with rich olive oil that the oil dripped down my cheeks, spilled on my clothes; I remembered the taste, the delicious, nutlike flavor unique to pure, freshly pressed olive oil. It was unbelievably good, and with more bread and some white wine the man who ran the press kept on hand, we had a jolly evening together.

That winter after Paco moved out, the press was closed because so few people were left to use it. There were only two thin lines of green wheat to relieve the gloom, and the neglected fields cried abandonment. Is it sad that old stone walls that served for centuries should crumble in uselessness? Only if you think it is sad. That a village that existed for centuries should die in a few years? Why shouldn't it? A village has a life and death like any other mortal thing. Eventually it is buried in ashes like Pompeii or destroyed in a war, or simply dies a natural death because it has no more reason to live, and the vital parts stop functioning.

"Hasn't been a new house built in my lifetime," the village mason used to grumble, "not one. Nothing but patching and fixing and shoring up the old ones. It's time there was some change, something new. New blood's what we need. Out with the old, I say, on with the new."

That spring, we learned what had happened to the Miro land. On the hillsides around the town and lining the approach to the village were the now familiar white stakes that announced the start of another development. People from Riera, looking for an escape from the dirt and noise of the town's new factories, were buying; people from Barcelona who could not afford the seashore and had persuaded themselves that mountain air was healthier anyhow were buying. Tiny houses began to spring up on tiny plots crowded with flowerpots.

The mason was as excited as a young boy seeing a circus come to town. At eighty-one, he was too old to be hired on the project, but he spent all day, every day, watching with satisfaction while machines cut deep gashes in the hills for roads, uprooted century-old almond and olive trees, and erected a network of thin, brick walls to enclose the lots. When we boarded up the house and went out the door for the last time that summer of 1971, just ten years after moving to the village, the once rich valley and surrounding hills were pockmarked with pert white bungalows, while Las Casas, in its somber dignity, was turning into a ruin on a hill.

The new development was called Las Casas, too, but it would never be a village. Las Casas del Torrente, my beloved village, was becoming a memory. Out with the old, on with the new, as the old mason said.